PARKED BY
THE EXIT

My Journey to Psychic Mediumship

Jackie Kenner

ISBN: 9798323250332

Cover design by: Jackie Kenner
Printed in the United States of America

Thank you:

Uncle TT, for taking a random message from a scared, confused, and desperate woman so many years ago. For responding with compassion, understanding, and a list of tools to pull myself from the depths of darkness.

My editors - Jocelyn Mackenzie, who very appropriately helped set the initial "tone" of this book. Agnes and Alex, for sticking by me through all iterations.

Neil and Moss for loving me endlessly and letting me love you right back. Bobo, Po, and Wa. Our family is a dream come true.

My mom. For letting me be.

And Spirit.

INTRODUCTION

For My Moss

I'm seventeen weeks pregnant at the time of starting this manuscript. I was married nineteen weeks ago. While I've always wanted to share the beautiful experiences of being a medium in a book, I never felt a sense of urgency until I became pregnant. Then I wanted to write for you, Moss, because this is a big, weird, and beautiful planet you're about to inhabit.

I want to help you learn and understand a few things that took me a long time to figure out. Mommy talks to dead people for a living, because we never really die. Our souls were somewhere before they came here, and they will continue on once our time here is done. Existing as various forms of light traveling endlessly throughout the cosmos.

No matter what anyone on this planet tries to convince you to believe, Mommy's truth is that who we are inside is the single most important thing about each and every one of us. How well we know this inner part of ourselves will impact every decision we make and every outcome we experience in this lifetime. I want you to ruthlessly search your inner world until you know every particle of your immaterial self. Because there is something hidden deep in there that is important to find. And I think it's hidden deep on purpose. Because the things we have to fight to find, we value. I hope you fight for it.

How close you are to your inner self will also determine the depths of your relationship with others. People who haven't taken a voyage through their inner world will be harder to connect with. I hope you have patience with them and find a way to love them anyway. But your true soul circle will be others who are searching the same way you're searching.

You will be here with us soon, gracing the planet, maybe even before I finish writing this manuscript—a journal of my deepest thoughts, memories, and lessons from my work as a medium and my path as a spiritual seeker.

I expect that someday when you're older, people may ask you about what Mommy does for a living. They may find it strange or even tease you. And I want to start you off with an important lesson on the ways of the world. Should you find yourself being questioned about your Mommy, remember this response.

You tell them, "My Daddy is weird too."

PREFACE

In the following chapters, I will use terms like Spirit (with a capitalized "S"), spirit, loving guidance, my guides, angels, the unseen, and the universe. While these are very different descriptive nouns, it's important to explain early on that I believe they all originate from the same energy source. They are a part of "Spirit," which is the single word I will use to encompass all of these terms.

I sometimes call my psychic connection "abilities" and sometimes call it a "gift." It is a gift to me in the same way experiencing life is a gift from the universe. There are many magical, incredibly beautiful sensations and experiences we get to have throughout our lifetimes. It's no oversight that there are also difficult, painful, or questionably unfair experiences. Considering my connection as a "gift" is a personal choice that is interwoven through my beliefs about what it means to live in the flesh. I'm not in the business of telling anyone else what to believe, but I do reserve my right to consider my connection a gift. I hope to share my perspective that we're all capable of experiencing some form of this gift.

I've made an effort to construct a timeline within this

book. My writing style, however, may occasionally lead the narrative to shift abruptly between moments, years, or possibly even realms. For the topic of mediumship, it's appropriate to release the constraints of linear storytelling. The Spirit world is fluid, boundless, and without time.

When I took on the task of writing a book about my experiences and memories, I felt compelled to organize my inner self in a manner I would never do in my everyday life. In my mind, memories exist within a vast and unstructured network. They are usually tucked away, without regard, but readily accessible when needed. There's a freedom in this unencumbered storage—memories simply float in my memory bank without categorization or order.

To write a book, I've forced and imposed structure upon these memories. I've had to categorize them, rank them, and put them in a sequential order for some kind of narrative to flow. This way, others who want to learn about my journey to mediumship can understand the process. The exercise of writing a book has oversimplified the complexities of my inner world.

I'm embarrassed to admit that I've written this book twice. The first time, I wrote the entire manuscript to completion. And I hated it. I edited the words over and over but something felt wrong about the entire thing. When I challenged myself to figure out why I disliked version one of the book, I had a breakthrough.

There have been a few prominent individuals throughout my life who doubted and belittled my psychic abilities. I was still trying to prove something to them through the words of the book. I envisioned them buying the book, reading my full story, and finally understanding how powerful my connection really is and how truly wrong they were about me. I'm not proud of that desire within myself.

But I realized that I didn't want to perpetuate this cycle any longer – the desire for acceptance from anyone other than my own spiritual self. It's not my responsibility to convince anyone of anything through this book. I know who and what I am in Spirit. I want to break free of what others think of me and simply tell the truth of my experiences. So I scrapped version one and started from the top. This time, not caring who believes what I share or how others perceive my connection to Spirit. As it pertains to the capabilities of our consciousness, I hope to reach readers who already "get it."

The following is my reality. All these things happened, whether any one individual finds them believable or not. Which is a liberating position to take–to simply share the truth. In version two of this book, I aim for my words to spark a similar soul liberation in those who come along on this journey with me.

BRACE FOR IMPACT

Deciding where to start is difficult. Where do I begin with something that has been an essential part of my existence for as long as I can remember? How do I clearly and orderly explain the intricacies of a psychic connection that has flickered on and off throughout my nearly four decades on this beautiful planet—sometimes dimmed by my own hand, other times by the unspoken pressure of society to conform to a mold of normalcy. A mold that simply doesn't fit.

Certain past events serve as undeniable evidence of my psychic development, the significance of which became apparent only in hindsight, sometimes many years later. It's scary for me to open up completely; to expose rawness and vulnerability by sharing the full spectrum of my experiences. In order to comprehend the boundless light and loving guidance of the spirit world, one must also confront the depths of darkness that exist in counterbalance. While I want to share the amazing impact of spiritual communication throughout my life, the truth is that it has unearthed layers of darkness and sadness that may have otherwise gone unknown.

To share my truth authentically means delving into every

aspect: the good and the bad, the light and the dark, the heavenly and the hellish.

Native American lore speaks of two great weavers, one sewing dark beads and the other, light. They compete endlessly in the eternal tapestry of life, striving to tip the balance toward purity or evil. This ongoing battle reflects what I've witnessed through my psychic connection— a timeless struggle between opposing forces of what we commonly refer to as good vs. evil.

Ultimately, we experience more of what we keep our focus on. And the deeper we grow in our spiritual understanding, the more we comprehend that both colors of beads have been created by the same beadmaker. The lightworkers of the world understand that it is not about outrunning the darkness, but instead, keeping our focus on our own endless light.

THE DISTANCE

The dim pre-dawn light cast long shadows across the quiet streets of Dallas as I approached the gym. It was 4:57 a.m. on a Tuesday morning, an ungodly hour to some, but the perfect time for my strength and conditioning class. Moss, my four-month-old son, was sleeping soundly at home. His father, my husband Neil, was lovingly keeping watch over him.

Entering the gym, I was greeted by the muted sounds of conversation as the coach and a few early risers chatted near the front. The air felt heavy with anticipation as we prepared for the day's workout. Despite the early hour, there was a sense of camaraderie among us, united by our shared commitment to fitness and self-improvement.

"Yeah, he's on forced resignation right now. An email went out to the entire school district this morning about it," the coach explained.

"About what?" I asked. It was clear I had missed a huge part of the story.

"One of his students came forward about his sexual advances towards her," a woman explained.

The coach chimed in, "Yep. Immediate termination. Well,

technically I guess he resigned, but they made him."

"It's disgusting," the same woman confirmed.

"Wait. Was he accused or has he been found guilty?" I questioned, legitimately wanting to get the details correct.

The atmosphere shifted subtly. I felt all eyes in the room turn towards me, their expressions a mixture of confusion and surprise. A heavy silence settled over us, thick with unspoken tension. Sensing the discomfort I had just caused, I waited for a response.

Finally, breaking the awkward silence, the woman spoke up. "The student has quite a solid story," she said, her words hanging in the air, laden with implication.

In that moment, it occurred to me that I had inadvertently stumbled into a conversation far weightier than I had anticipated. It took a second for the impact of my ignorance to register and I suddenly felt exposed, vulnerable, and misunderstood.

I learned that a teacher in a nearby school district had been accused of sexual advances by one of his students and that the school had mandated an immediate resignation.

"Ah, right. Okay," I muttered awkwardly, attempting to brush off my discomfort as I set my belongings down and moved to claim my spot on the gym floor. I was desperate to escape the scrutiny I felt in the room.

I settled into my spot for class, a whirlwind of self-doubt

disturbed me. I was aware of my ability to be naively socially awkward. My discomfort lingered, distracting my focus before the class. I knew that accusations could be false and that they could cost a life. A truth that I assume none of my counterparts at the gym were considering in the slightest.

Lost in my thoughts, I considered the innocence of my inquiry. And despite my intentions, the reality remained that I had unwittingly breached a social boundary.

I had been a professionally practicing medium for over a decade at that point. My experiences with the spirit world had created a widening gap between myself and other "normal" individuals. The more immersed I became in bridging the realms of the physical and the metaphysical, the more isolated I felt from mainstream society. I was able to see and understand much more about earthly situations from the perspective of passed spirits.

We started the workout as a group. I was still overthinking my question. My fellow workout buddies had all long moved forward from our conversation. Because they knew nothing of the tragic tale of Logan, a young man from New Zealand who had taken his own life in the darkness of night. He hung himself from a tree outside his mother's bedroom window. Logan was all I could think about. My friends were peacefully oblivious to the soul-shattering ramifications of a false accusation, unaware of the anguish it could inflict on an innocent soul.

They didn't know the depths of despair that I had witnessed during my medium session with Logan's mother just one week prior—the heart-wrenching agony that overcame her as she grieved the loss of her son and the outcome of unfounded accusations. Or how I had fought to maintain composure throughout the session, struggling to hold back tears until I could no longer bear the burden alone. I had completed the session, then woke my husband moments after to seek solace in his embrace as I wept at the cruelty of the world. And this early morning, I still hadn't shaken the emotional toll of Logan's medium session.

Existing socially as a psychic medium is a challenge. It's too uncomfortable to bear all–to explain my "odd" questions or why I sometimes take the positions I take socially. It's far too awkward to pause a conversation and share a dark story about why I am the way I am. Nor what I've seen from the other side. There are depths of darkness that most people don't want to hear about.

I continued on with my workout that morning in the gym, accepting that I probably came across as tone deaf in asking my truly innocent question. And that just like many other moments in my life, I would likely never have the time or space to explain myself to my peers.

LOGAN

B ut I get to explain myself here. The following story is emotionally devastating. It's one of the most difficult sessions I've ever led. It encompasses many genuinely challenging topics: the harmful sides of social media, the damaging impact of accusations, the difficulties of adolescence, suicide, and posthumous messages from spirits that are agonizing to share.

It's led me to worry deeply about the younger generation, who have never experienced life apart from their on-screen avatars. As we move forward in time, humanity will be increasingly interwoven with the digital realm, artificial intelligence, and virtual representations of ourselves online. Will the generations ahead of us even understand that their true identity and worth in life can exist independently from their online presence?

Logan failed to grasp this concept. He couldn't comprehend that his digital persona could exist in a separate reality, distinct and aligned with the truth of who he really was. So he ended his physical life.

My relationship with the spirit of Logan started with a calendar notification of a booking at 9:00 p.m. This often meant that the client lived in another country. I had intentionally kept late-night spaces available on my calendar for people in distant time zones. Coincidentally, on that particular evening, I had plans for a taco dinner with girlfriends, an engagement I had regrettably forgotten to block off in my calendar.

I considered the conflicting schedule dilemma. When something like this happens with a session or even a session request, I turn inward to seek guidance, asking for loving insight on the best course of action. Should I reschedule the session? Cancel my taco dinner? Maybe I could compromise by leaving the dinner early to take the session? My gut told me to keep the scheduled appointment. I felt a heaviness for this one, and believed that I could help the most by keeping it at the scheduled time. I often get senses about sessions the second I see the booking confirmation. Sometimes even just reading the client's name in the appointment notification I receive on my smartphone will initiate contact with the energy of both the client and the spirit.

I joined the taco dinner with my friends and warned them that I would need to leave early for "work." Despite my decade-long tenure as a practicing medium, discussing my profession was still a delicate topic, even among my closest friends. Conversations about communicating with the deceased are avoided or met with discomfort. The concept of mediumship can carry a taboo stigma. Many view my connection with the dead as forbidden or associate it with dark magic. I've grown to accept that my work is unlikely something I'll ever share openly about in my circle of friends.

I was not myself throughout the dinner. I felt a heaviness

overtaking me. I kept seeing a spirit that looked similar to my own nephew. He had fair skin and light hair, a quirky flair to his personality, and was attempting to show me multiple cooking projects. The resemblance to my nephew was so uncanny that I couldn't help but wonder if I was just thinking of my nephew for some inexplicable reason.

I left the dinner much earlier than I had planned. I wanted to get home to start my pre-session process. About an hour before my scheduled session start time, I open myself to the spirit world, going through my connection process, then asking Spirit to show me only what is highest and best for my client to receive during our time together. I dedicate myself to connecting from a place of light and love, inviting forth the ultimate truth for the client's spiritual and emotional growth and well-being. As I settle into this meditative state, I write down every impression and insight that comes to me, compiling a list of information to draw upon once our session begins. I have this list prepared before a single word is even exchanged.

As I entered my focused state, the same spirit that I had sensed at the taco dinner made his presence known once again. He appeared young, perhaps in his late teens, radiating a glowing energy that drew me in. I found myself developing a deep fondness for him. His demeanor was sweet and somewhat shy. He was showing me playful visions of cooking and types of pastries that he liked to make. Specifically, he was flashing through visions of licking the stirring spoon. Each vision and impression carried a sense of warmth and sweetness that was endearing to me.

Feeling confident in the pre-session connection, I began the call with a sense of readiness. I discovered that it was Logan's mother, Stacy, who had arranged the call. I got right into it, sharing with her everything that I had intuited. I told her about the strong presence of her son and that he had been coming to me for the entire afternoon leading up to our meeting. As I described my impressions to her, she listened attentively, confirming that my words resonated deeply and that it "sounded exactly like him."

"He's a little shy," I shared with her. "I get a feeling I can't put my finger on. It's almost like he's embarrassed."

"Well, I could see that," she admitted. "He was my only son, and he took his own life."

Sharing the full details from another's session is not something I've ever taken liberties with. It means the world to me to protect the privacy of my clients and their sacred messages from the other side. But there are parts of this conversation that I feel in my soul are important to make known on this earth. This is my retelling of what was covered in our call together, not Stacy's. It is a combination of what Stacy shared with me, what Logan showed me, and what the loving guidance around all of us taught me. But I have stripped it back to mostly facts, allowing the most tender details to remain anonymously secure between Stacy and Logan.

Logan had recently completed high school, a milestone marked by his acceptance of a rugby scholarship abroad. With plans to embark on this exciting journey, he was on the cusp of a new chapter in his life. But the summer before he would leave for his studies, a disturbing event unfolded. One of Logan's closest friends took to social media to make a shocking allegation against him. This accusation was harsh, and it cast a dark shadow over what should have been a time of celebration and anticipation for Logan's future endeavors.

Tragically, Logan found himself energetically buried by the digital accusation, unable to break free from its grip. Consumed by the relentless scrutiny and condemnation of others on social media, he spiraled into a state of obsession, plagued by self-doubt and a profound sense of worthlessness. As the rumor spread like wildfire, he struggled with the terrible notion that he was irredeemably tainted, destined to be forever defined by this unfounded allegation.

One evening, about six months before our call, in the quiet of the night, Stacy woke up to go to the bathroom. She bumped into Logan in the hallway, which surprised both of them. Worried about why he was awake so late, she asked if he needed anything. But Logan just brushed her off, saying he was watching a show on his laptop. Despite an uneasy gut-feeling, Stacy went back to bed, ignoring a deeper concern that something was off.

She awoke the next morning to her husband's panicked voice, his face drained of color and filled with distress. He informed her that something terrible had happened, that the ambulance had arrived, and she needed to come to the backyard immediately. Rushing to the scene in her robe, she stepped onto the back porch and was confronted with the horrifying sight of her son's lifeless body hanging from the tree.

The paramedics carefully lowered his body from the tree to the ground, tenderly wrapping him in a sleeping bag. With compassionate concern, they approached the devastated mother, asking if she would like to spend a little more time with her son before they took him away. She told me that she lay beside him, on the ground, for quite some time.

I'm not afraid to shed tears alongside my clients; it's a natural expression of empathy and connection. In fact, it's quite common for me to do so. I'm determined not to develop emotional calluses that would dull my sensitivity to both the spirits' and my clients' emotions. However, in this particular case, I couldn't afford to let my feelings out. It would not be just a gentle release of tears. It felt like a dam breaking, with an overwhelming surge of emotions threatening to overtake me.

Maybe it was the striking resemblance to my nephew, or perhaps it was Logan's gentle spirit that touched me so deeply. It could have been the daunting realization that I was bringing my own son into a world fraught with digital dangers. I was a new mom to a few-month-old baby boy myself. But above all, I was haunted by the stark truth that I strongly believed Logan's accuser was lying. The accuser's deceit had led to the tragic loss of a young life. And then there was the heart-wrenching image of that final goodbye, the devastating scene beneath the tree in their backyard. The senselessness and needless tragedy of it all tore at my soul. I could feel Stacy's anguish reverberating through every fiber of my being.

By the end of the session, despite the difficulty, I felt an overwhelming gratitude towards the spirit world, extending from the depths of my soul, for granting me the gift of connection if only for this one person–this devastated mother. Her son was okay on the other side. And he had been waiting patiently, wishing to talk with her.

Before concluding the call, I asked permission to share one more detail we hadn't yet covered. Stacy graciously agreed.

"Did your son enjoy cooking?" I inquired.

"Oh, absolutely," she replied. "He made pastries all the time, and he absolutely loved to lick the spoon."

This story is just one of the many heart-wrenching sessions I've experienced with clients over the years. I've chosen to share this one in particular because it's a pertinent example of how who I am today has been shaped by the confronting and difficult conversations I've had with the other side. Through Logan's story, I learned at least one profound lesson: accusations aren't always facts. This is a perspective that often sets me apart in a culture of fast finger-pointing and hasty judgment.

Of course, I'm aware that my connection could have been wrong. Maybe my wires got crossed and I misperceived something. "What if he did do it?" you may find yourself wondering. These are normal contemplations and something I don't shy away from thinking over. I have to leave space within myself for inaccuracies and be okay with the possibility of mistakes happening. And while I don't personally feel that I misread anything in Logan's case, I still hold fast to the life lesson I inherited from this connection. Accusations aren't facts. And they can ruin someone's life.

Throughout my journey as a psychic medium, I've encountered no spirit that remained inaccessible on the "other side." I have never encountered a (human) soul lingering in limbo, seeking assistance to transition to the afterlife. Every soul, irrespective of the circumstances of their passing or the quality of their earthly existence, finds its way to the same destination. Even those who commit suicide.

All spirits make their way to a realm of profound enlightenment, where they focus on and commit to continual healing, growth, and spiritual ascension. While souls are capable of honest reflection, they don't seem to have a judgment system the way we do as humans. Meaning, they don't categorize things as "good" or "bad," but instead reflect on areas of needed growth and healing. They are not hard on themselves.

In Logan's case, he wasn't ashamed of his choices, but he was careful and somewhat timid in approaching how he had caused his mother to feel. This had registered as feeling "embarrassed" to me. He wanted to connect with her to recognize that he hadn't considered the amount of pain he would cause her, but instead was overly focused on his own suffering. These kinds of "last words" between the living and the departed can offer a great deal of healing.

The desire of spirits is often to reach out to their earthly relatives, guiding them toward paths of divine joy, assisting them in not repeating generational mistakes, and encouraging them to connect to their deepest inner selves. They almost always wish to comfort those left behind and to assure the loved ones on earth that they knew they were loved. And that they are okay on the other side, enjoying all the pastry spoons they want.

BURRITO BABY

A few months after my session with Logan, my husband and I were dining on the patio at one of our favorite Vietnamese spots in a trendy neighborhood of Dallas. It was a sunny but cool day, especially when the wind picked up. We had our son, Moss, with us and I was worried that the wind was going to give him a chill.

I took a swaddling blanket from the diaper bag and rolled it around Moss. As we waited for our order, I started dancing around the patio with Moss to keep him entertained. We were the only patrons out there and I had space and privacy to move about freely. I often make up silly songs for Moss on the fly. My husband calls them my "show tunes".

As I spun around quickly, a move that always makes Moss giggle, I began to sing ad-lib, "He's a burrito baby, portaling through the galaxy, the galaxy, the galaxy. He's a burrito baby, portaling everywhere."

I finished with a jump on the final word. Moss was squealing with delight and my husband was laughing at the two of us, a beautiful vision of adoration, as he basked in the golden sunlight. In the middle of one of the sweetest moments I'd experienced in our newly formed family, a darkness overtook me. It was instant and inexplicable.

I thought of Logan, swaddled in a sleeping bag. His mother's love. The heaviness of sorrow and grief. I envisioned Logan's soul portalling throughout the expanse of the unseen. I felt guilty about both my uninitiated provocation of this terrible memory and at the fact that I could squeeze my very much alive and happy baby.

There's a surprise factor to being a psychic medium in a physical body. I cannot always control the biological functions sustaining my humanness. My body stores vibrational memories that can be triggered and instantaneously dislodged into my awareness, especially if the memories are painful and unresolved or unprocessed. To state it simply, I can't "unconnect" from what I have connected to through my sessions. And while I do my best to process the emotions I experience during my mediumship, sometimes they creep up on me in the most unexpected times. In this instance, the contrast was altogether confusing. We were having such a special moment. Thinking of Logan at this very second just didn't make any sense to me.

Telepathically, I began to apologize to both Logan and Stacy for my thoughts. I visualized my words reaching their spiritual essences through the ethereal connections we all share. I tried to keep a facade of lightness on my external composure, ashamed to confess to my husband everything going on inside of me right then and there.

"I'm so sorry. I can't believe this is what I'm thinking about right now," I said to Logan's soul, somewhere out there.

"It's beautiful," I heard Logan say back, his spirit appearing bright and pure. "You're beautiful," he added. "Enjoy these moments. I am happy here on the other side. And this love is stunning to watch."

WHAT'S HAPPENING PHYSICALLY AND MENTALLY

What exactly is happening to me when I am making a mediumship connection? In my physical body, it doesn't feel like much changes for me. Though I have seen recordings of myself connecting and noticed that my eyes begin to make short, rapid movements. I wasn't aware of this eye movement until I watched myself—and it's clearly observable. Once I became aware of it, I wanted to understand what was going on while my eyes were doing this. Surely it would be hard to visually focus. How could I never have noticed this?

The next time I led a mediumship session after witnessing the eye motions, I tried to pay attention to what was going on with my visual focus when this movement began. I realized that I wasn't using my vision at all. I wasn't focusing my eyes on anything. Even though my eyes were open and rapidly moving, I was not "seeing" the world around me because I was entirely focused elsewhere. I was tuning into the unseen. The most similar thing I could compare this to is when we're intensely focused on a mental task and we don't notice the sounds around us–perhaps for even minutes at a time. But then we break our deep focus, and all of the sudden we hear the sounds that were there the whole time. When we were fixated on our thoughts, we simply had no connection to the input from our audio sensing.

This has ended up being a funny, recurring theme in my marriage because this intense focus state happens for me outside of my medium sessions as well. I can be looking right at my husband's face while simultaneously extremely deep in thought. He will be talking to me and I simply won't register his voice or the meaning of his words.

"Jackie, are you hearing anything I'm saying," he'll ask.

And then I tune back into my audio input and apologize for my distraction. I'm not sure if this intense focus is unique to mediums–but I do think it's a "type" of focus style.

I have a dear friend who jokes that my mind is like a laser. While I may often have twenty-seven simultaneous channels going at once, when I elect to tune into one channel, it's a laser-like focus that is difficult to break. All other twenty-seven channels may as well be non-existent. I suspect there are others like me who "tune in" this way. And who knows; they may make for the best psychics.

I have also noticed that my breathing gets shallower and more rapid when I am making medium connections. This is involuntary, in that I pay no mind to my breathing patterns when I connect. I'm aware of existing research around intentional, rhythmic breathwork leading to enhanced mental states, but I've never attempted to make sense of my breath change. It is not something I've trained or even realized was happening for the first ten years of my mediumship practice.

There are other physical reactions when I connect, but they occur when I am trying to suppress the connection as opposed to when I am intentionally tuning in. Sharing my contract with the spirit world will help explain these symptoms of suppressed connection.

I do not live my life consciously tapped into other people's energy privacy. In other words, no, I am not "reading" people all the time. And I'm definitely not reading anyone's mind. Which is something I've been told people fear about psychics. The truth is, I'm pretty wrapped up in my own thoughts most of the time. I think that the majority of us are and that this tendency to be self-focused is simply human nature. We have lives we need to live and things we need to do that take up our mental load.

But I have made a personal contract with the spirit world. My contract is that I do not connect for anyone unless they have booked a session with me, because this booking is their way of granting me permission to tune into their energy. We all have an energy field around us. And through that field, I can access past loved ones who are connected in spirit, loving guidance readily available for that individual, energy distortions that are affecting the highest and best life for that individual, and archetypal (or past life) patterns that are present. The archetypal patterns appear as strengths that we come into this life with, and if we can tune into those strengths, we can do really amazing things. For example, I have a strong "teacher" pattern that I acknowledge and live out by sharing about the spiritual world to help others create their own connections.

Every one of us has guides. People want to know who or what their guides are, and what to call them. This is not something I can decipher for another. I can share how I see someone else's guides, but I am not an authority of the spirit world. Chances are, your guides will appear for you much differently than they appear for me. We'll get into guides much more in later chapters.

Then there is a second form of consent that I accept, and that is someone asking me in conversation if I sense anything or anyone around them. In both scenarios, my connection has been asked for and is therefore not intrusive. I really don't want to engage in other people's private lives without their request. But, I have one exception.

The exception is that I have agreed with Spirit to share a medium connection with someone if it's critical to get a message to them–even if they haven't booked with me and they haven't asked me to connect. And I've agreed to this through what I call "my contract." I don't get to determine what critical means and I don't always get to know why a message is coming through or the impact it has on the receiver.

How do I determine if something is critical? First, if I sense a spirit or see a shadow, I first ask if the presence is there for me or someone else. If it's for me, I engage. If it's for someone else and I do not recognize the spirit, I simply tell them "no." I remind myself and the spirit that I am not "working" at that moment and that the person they're trying to reach hasn't asked for my help. Most of the time, if I sense a deceased loved one around someone and I tell the loved one, or the spirit, "no," they will go. Spirits are indescribably compassionate and considerate presences. And while they are typically excited to make connections, I have always felt a sense of kindness from them because they typically honor my desire to live a mostly normal life and not go around connecting for strangers all the time.

But occasionally I tell the spirits no, and the connection amplifies. This is when more physical symptoms show up. I feel the urge to press my lips together. And sometimes I start scrunching my nose. This is something I've observed in Teresa Caputo, the Long Island Medium. I couldn't say if I saw her do it and then did it myself or if it's just something some mediums do when they are feeling a spirit. I was watching Teresa Caputo on television long before I understood that I am a medium. I make these movements in my face to try to bring my focus and awareness back to my physical body.

When I say no and the connection amplifies, I typically just leave the area. I wish I was so bold as to approach a stranger when the spirit is trying this hard, but I usually just can't do it. It's too awkward and I never want to force something like this on someone. There is also a possibility that they will think I am evil. Extreme as that may seem, a lot of people believe psychics and psychic mediums are working with dark magic, the occult, or witchcraft.

Rather than run the risk of public ridicule, I typically opt to just leave the area. On occasion, even when I've left, the spirit doubles down on their attempt. This is when I know that I am "under contract." And when I sense the spirit world this intensely, the final physical symptom is that I start to cry. They're not tears of sadness, but instead, they are tears of simple release. I'm feeling so much that I would describe it as sensory overload, and my body creates tears as a way to rebalance itself.

If the spirit stays with me beyond saying no and leaving, only then will I approach the person I believe the spirit is attempting to reach. I always start by explaining that I am a psychic medium and asking if they are open to receiving a message from the other side.

If this were me, and someone approached me randomly and asked to give me a medium message, I'd feel instantaneously two very extreme ways. One, I'd question their connection and worry that they are not legit. Two, I'd be excited and desperately want to know anything and everything about what they were getting from the unseen realms.

I can understand when people tell me no, which they do about half of the time. They don't know me from a bar of soap. They certainly don't know what I'm connected to or if I have their best interests at heart. In addition to that, I'm typically seemingly emotional by this point, with tears in my eyes. I could imagine that my appearance comes across as unstable to a complete stranger.

This contract is something I established over the years. It was my decision to consent to "random" connections under certain circumstances with defined parameters. I learned that I can create rules for visiting spirits. If they tell me something in a session that is too vague or difficult to interpret, I tell them that if they want me to do something with what they're showing me, they need to make it more clear. Otherwise, I am unable to translate the vision and I will move on. In the same manner, I established rules with visiting spirits. If after three attempts to shut down their connection the intensity increases, I have agreed through my personal contract to approach a stranger.

This kind of intensity from the spirit world is infrequent and I don't mind honoring my contract. In my first decade of mediumship, this happened to me less than a handful of times. Typically, as I'm saying no, I remind the spirit world that they can work with that person to nudge them to book a session with a medium. I try to put some of the pressure back on the spirit because I do believe that our deceased loved ones can influence our decision to seek out a medium.

This can show up suddenly. We may start to think of our loved one more often or people often report that they started to have dreams of their passed loved ones leading up to their booking. Sometimes clients will tell me that they were considering booking a session and then all these little synchronicities started happening–like their song came on the playlist more than once, or that they came across a photo or a note out of nowhere. I think these are ways that the spirit world can entice us to seek out connections with them.

If you're wondering what's in the contract for me, the spirit world does have its end of the bargain to uphold. I have agreed to do this work provided they continue to make my path in life clear, easy, and guided towards what's highest and best for my soul's growth. While I'm being cute in stating this, I also sometimes remind spirits how loyal I am to them and my connection when I need to ask special favors. An example of this was the first time my son got sick–I requested that they facilitate a quick and painless healing for him and threw in the gentle reminder of how many times I'd gone above and beyond for them. While I'm partially teasing in my request, there is a part of me that also hopes that we get some kind of karmic clout when we're diligent and loyal spiritual lightworkers.

The physical effects of mediumship connection for me are way more straightforward to describe than the non-physical process I'm going through–what's happening inside of me. I don't think the medium connection is mental, so much as spiritual. I think the mind, or mental processing, is the channel through which psychic mediums make sense of our connection and then we relay it back through verbal language to a human being sitting opposite of us as the client.

I see individuals on earth as massive energy beings that embody a physical form for some time before ultimately returning to spiritual form. Their energy bodies and the connection that these bodies have to other realms is what makes medium connections possible. To describe the soul or spirit as being "in the body" is not actually the way I observe things. The spirit is with the body and parts of it are "in" the body, but our spirits are much larger than our bodies. And they're not a static shape, color, or size. They are more like fluid, luminescent energy forms that flow within a greater cosmic web. And within this greater web, which traverses infinite realms, we can connect to our guides, teachers, higher selves, and loved ones.

WHAT SPIRITS LOOK LIKE

I magine a plasma orb, glowing brilliant, pearlescent shades of light akin to the glow of a neon sign. They are not one color; they're a swirling amoeba of multiple, brilliant colors. Shades of pastel yellow, purples, blues, and greens. Those are the colors I've seen in the souls that I've encountered so far. They look unbelievable, as there's nothing on this planet to truly liken them to. The closest thing on earth would be the Northern Lights or bioluminescent waters—both natural phenomena that humans travel thousands of miles to observe. We stand in complete awe of their beauty, their seemingly impossible existence. I propose that a part of us is taken aback by them because they remind a deeper part of us of a time and place that we were in before our existence on Earth.

Now imagine these luminescent qualities in a starform—somewhat spherical. And somehow they're both massive and miniscule at the same time, ever-changing. This is the most accurate description I could give of the way I see spirits.

When I'm having a medium connection, that part of who I am is connecting with that part of who the deceased loved one is. We're not using words. The speed of information transmission is amplified; it's instantaneous. Verbalizing through language like we do on earth is slow compared to communication with spirit. A mediumship connection is a transfer of every particle of thought, memory, vision, and emotion. I end up writing a lot down during sessions. I want to remember everything I can about the transfer from spirit to share with my client, and the client and I often begin talking about one part of the message before I can relay the full message in its totality.

The spirits do, however, identify themselves. They sometimes do this by showing me how they appeared on earth in the lifetime relevant to the client. I don't want to get too tricky here, but I do believe we have many lifetimes. If my client is asking to connect to her husband, the spirit might show itself as a tall male wearing overalls and carrying a box but still exists as the light orb.

"Oh, yes!" my client will say. "He went fishing every weekend and he only wore overalls when he fished. He was six-foot-five, so yes, that's him."

This is just a cute little detail, but sometimes spirits want me to tell the client about how they "look" and will ask me to point out a beautiful feature. I might say something like, "She keeps showing me her curly hair. She wants you to know about her curly hair."

The client may then explain that the passed loved one had lost all of her hair a few months before passing and was devastated because she loved her curls.

Spirits don't always use physical features. Sometimes they'll show me a memory, specific item, gesture, or even exact word to help the client trust that they are truly connected. This will be something that there's just no way I could possibly know. Were I to run a Google search or attempt online research, these details are not something that would turn up.

Sometimes, especially when the client and spirit are from another culture, I cannot make sense of the item they are using to identify themselves. I was once working with a woman who had lost her father. I told her that her dad was showing me Christmas ornaments on strings, almost like a necklace. This didn't make sense to either one of us at the time, but when she went home that evening and shared this with her mother, the mom knew exactly what they were. They were Argentinian Bolas, which do look much like Christmas ornaments on strings. They are used to entangle livestock by throwing them toward the running animal's legs, and are often thrown by a cowboy on horseback. The client's father was a rancher and had his grandfather's Bolas, which the mother had kept and cherished since the father's passing. They were a family heirloom.

When I can't make sense of what I'm seeing like the Bolas, I suggest that the client keep it in the back of their mind. Especially when the client can't make sense of it either. I ask them to suspend judgment and just allow themselves to stay open to what might be trying to come through. Oftentimes we won't know what something means initially, but as the session continues, all of a sudden the client remembers! Sometimes I get a text or email long after the session has concluded from a client sharing that they finally figured out exactly what it was that I was seeing.

I was working with a woman over the phone once and told her that her mother was trying to show me something by the remote controls. It was blue and white and looked like it had plastic around it. The client checked all the remote controls in her house and said it didn't make sense, and that she couldn't find anything like what I was describing. After we ended our session, she sent me a photo of what she saw nearby almost immediately after we hung up.

In the photo was a wooden dish on the floor beside two blue and white lamps wrapped in bubble wrap. The wooden dish was what my client used to store her TV remotes in and the lamps on the floor were a wedding gift from her mother that she hadn't found the heart to unwrap and use since the mother's passing. She said she had just moved the remote dish over there while cleaning earlier that day and hadn't put it back where it belonged yet. Because her mom wasn't using exact words when she was connecting with me, I could not get the precise details correct—but it made sense later!

Sometimes spirits do use exact words, especially if they were known for using a peculiar saying or the specific word has a deep meaning for the client. I was working with a client in Puerto Rico who wanted to know if her grandmother had any messages for her. I told her that I kept hearing "esperanza," which was a word I couldn't remember the translation for but knew from my years studying Spanish throughout my education.

"That's so perfect," my client explained. "I keep seeing grasshoppers on my balcony and they make me think of her. I have this little thing she gave me with a grasshopper on it and the word esperanza is written below it."

I was working with an Italian family once that wanted to connect with a recently passed male relative. I kept telling them that he was talking about something like "tha britches," which is a Southern dialect word for pants. I was up north in Maine so it didn't make any sense to me. And every time I said it, the family would roll with laughter. They explained to me that they believed he was saying "abbracci," which is Italian for "hugs." This was something he would say over and over anytime someone planned to leave. He wanted lots and lots of hugs.

One of my favorite forms of communication from spirits is when they show me a gesture or a memory. I get to see the scene unfold and feel the feelings that were being experienced. An example of a gesture came through when I was working with a client who had lost her aunt.

"She keeps showing me something like smooshing a marshmallow. And she's using that word like 'smoosh' and squeezing it."

The client explained that the aunt's nickname for her was similar to "smoosh" and that she would say it every time they greeted each other while pinching her cheeks gently. The aunt wanted me to tell the niece that she was doing that from the other side. And I could feel her deep love for her daughter–the way she cherished everything about her. I relay these emotions to the clients because I think I would want to know them if I were in the client's shoes, especially when they are so deep and loving.

When I am able to connect with these souls, they present themselves to me with attributes and memories so that I can relay these identifiers and my clients will recognize them and have a sense of trust in their connection. This is true for a spirit who may have passed a few weeks ago, but the same is true for someone who passed decades ago.

It's easy for me to share the details of my spirit communication—how spirits identify themselves, how they show items, gestures, memories etc. But the process of what is happening inside of me is admittedly a little beyond me.

I think this is something that has baffled humans for quite some time. There have been countless studies of psychic phenomena. You can find thousands of books and research papers from the early 1900s when scientists began taking a particular interest in the psychic mind. And while all of the studies were undisputedly able to observe psychic phenomena, not a single one of them was able to explain the how. But regardless, it's happening.

HOW IT HAPPENS

We receive text messages and emails on our wireless devices. But how many of us could explain the true technical side of this process? We know it involves intangible wavelengths and complex technology. But we don't typically think about the implications beyond that functionality. At best, we're okay with the fact that invisible, understandable messages are sent through the æther. We simply use our convenient devices and move on, rarely, if ever pausing to consider that they are proof that imperceivable communications can be transmitted with the right technology. I couldn't explain the ultimate mechanics of how being a medium works. I just receive the "texts", so to speak, and share them with my clients.

This contact with spirits can sometimes start with a moving shadow. I'll be going about my typical day, doing routine things with my mental processing state somewhere between focused and slightly in what is called flow state. Imagine the feeling when you're in the shower. You're focused enough to wash your body, but your thoughts have sort of drifted into a place slightly outside of controlled awareness. And the thoughts start taking on a life of their own for a split second. You're not really thinking about the thoughts, nor are you thinking about your tasks. It can happen when you're doing chores, cleaning up, or anything where you already "know the drill" enough to slip into a more relaxed mental mode. Then I'll feel my husband or my pet enter the room and see the light change due to their physical matter crossing the path between me and the light. I see the light change and my body makes me aware that someone is present. Anyone can usually sense when someone enters the same room as us, even if we're not looking at them. But when I turn to look at who I believe has entered the room, I see only a fleeting shadow. The shadow moves quickly and disappears upward.

I know when this happens that I have two options. Option one is to question myself and what I saw. Maybe someone did enter the room but then they left before I turned around? I still sometimes try to convince myself of this, even though I saw something dissipate into the ceiling. Option two is to engage. I recommend engaging with the spirit world with questions. Because we get what we ask for. More on that later.

"Who are you here for? Who are you?" I ask, sometimes telepathically and sometimes out loud.

These are my starting questions because it's important to clarify if a visitor is here for me or someone else. I don't like this truth about myself, but I've hosted enough medium sessions that I sometimes forget clients. I just flat out can't remember almost anything about them after enough time passes. It's not that I don't care about my clients, because I truly do. In fact, I was taught to find the "God" in each and every one of them and I make it my mission to do so during every single session I host. But after enough time has passed and enough other sessions have built up in between, it becomes nearly impossible to keep track of it all.

But I don't forget spirits. They have a unique "signature" that never leaves me once I've tuned in. Because they don't just show up as a face, like running into someone at a coffee shop that you just know you know but you can't remember how. Their face is familiar but you cannot for anything recall how you recognize them. But spirits come through more like a package of all the things we talked about in our session and all the symbols and visuals they shared to identify themselves. And when they do come through, I immediately remember the client they came for.

I try to track down the client when this happens to tell them how much effort their loved one is making to try to get a message through to them. Because it is difficult for the spirit world to make us aware of them, even with a medium like myself and especially when I am not intentionally initiating communication as I do in my sessions.

The first time I saw a shadow-figure, before I knew this was a sign of a visiting spirit for me, I was volunteering at a pottery studio in the Hell's Kitchen neighborhood of New York City. I was able to use the studio space in exchange for my volunteer service two nights a month. As I was cleaning up one evening, I felt one of the staff approach the sink beside me. From the corner of my eye, I saw that it was Gary and I started talking to him. When I turned to make eye contact, there was no one there. I took a step back, feeling both confused and consumed by shock.

The owner of the studio approached me, concerned, "Are you okay, Jackie?"

"You're going to think this is crazy. But I just saw a ghost. Like almost in the flesh. But it was from the corner of my eye, so not focused. And it had the exact mannerisms of Gary. Like I was talking to Gary but then I turned to look at him and I was actually alone."

The owner clearly wasn't making as much of the happening as I was. He just shrugged, kind of laughed, and responded under his breath, "Yeah, well. Gary had a twin brother that died. It really crushed him. Never talks about it."

And then he just walked off like nothing. But I was disturbed. In fact, I don't think I got my bearings for the rest of the evening. I saw the twin in spirit form.

When my psychic abilities started to amplify throughout my early to mid-twenties, it was challenging for me to come to grips with this new reality. I was experiencing things that "just couldn't be." But they very much were —they were happening, that's for sure. And what's odd about these psychic breakthroughs is that I would often stay in denial or self doubt that they were real. Which is a maddening phase to endure; trying to convince yourself that your own experiences aren't reality. At some point, there had been enough occurrences that I gave myself permission to accept them. There were too many accuracies and I just couldn't dismiss them anymore. It took me several months to believe myself that I had seen

Gary's brother's spirit at the pottery shop.

Over time, I've come to accept that I do sometimes see shadow figures when a spirit is trying to make contact. And now they don't disturb me in the slightest. I've even become comfortable enough with my husband to tell him when I see them. Sometimes we laugh because I'll first check and see if he saw something too.

I mentioned that I think it takes a lot of energy for spirits to materialize, even into shadow form. The majority of the time, spirits and I are communicating through a type of thought-wave, which is easy–effortless even. There is no physical manifestation of the spirit in most of my medium sessions. It's my understanding that making an impact on the physical realm, such as producing a shadow, takes a lot of effort from spirits. It's my personal belief that this substantial energetic undertaking indicates these spirits need and want to make connections.

An aunt that I loved dearly passed in her sleep sometime between noon and one o'clock in the afternoon. On that same day, as I was doing typical household chores, I saw a shadow figure not once, but twice. I was preoccupied with my tasks and didn't give it much thought. I just took a mental note and assumed that I was going to hear from a new client soon. A few hours later, when my family called to tell me of her passing, I immediately thought of the shadow. I believe it was her trying to get my attention. And of course, I regret that I didn't follow my own recommended protocol to ask who it was and who they were there for. But I know in my heart it was her, and I'd like to believe she was giving me a spirit-wink on the way out. She would have found this book really neat. But as I tell my clients, she can see it all from where she is.

◆ In addition to physically seeing shadows, there is another symptom of mediumship connection worth noting. Either during or right before sessions with clients, I often sense the circumstances surrounding the spirits's passing. For instance, if someone suffered a heart attack, I might feel tightness in my chest. Similarly, if they had a stomach condition, I might experience intense discomfort to the point of feeling nauseous. Interestingly, these sensations aren't always related to the deceased spirit. Sometimes, I pick up on the ailments of the client booking the session. For example, my right knee could start hurting in the morning and by the 3:00 pm session, the pain is so severe that I believe I need to see a specialist. However, when I ask the client about any knee pain, they reveal that they recently underwent surgery on that knee. Despite my years of mediumship experience, I still occasionally forget that the pain may not be mine but rather a result of an energetic connection to the client. My husband bears the brunt of my pre-session ailments. He chuckles when my sessions end and I report back that I am fine and the pain has subsided.

This phenomenon is unsettling when I don't have a session scheduled. Even if I remember to check if the sensation is actually mine or related to an upcoming session, there's no client or spirit to attribute it to.

One Thanksgiving, several years into my mediumship practice, I was getting ready to join my then-boyfriend and his family for a celebratory meal. As the day progressed, I found myself becoming increasingly emotionally unsettled. I was unable to stabilize my feelings, oscillating between deep grief and uncontrollable crying. Eventually, I had to admit to my boyfriend that I didn't believe I could keep myself together and sit through this family meal we had planned for weeks. Behavior like this was completely out of character for me, and I felt embarrassed and ashamed to cancel such an important event with no clear explanation. I have a personal motto to "honor my commitments," and it's a principle I adhere to without fail.

My boyfriend had left for his parent's house and I was alone in our apartment, feeling lost and confused. I lit a candle and made myself a cup of tea, trying to calm both my nerves and my racing thoughts. "What is wrong with you?" I wondered, unable to make sense of my own emotions or the sudden need to cancel such plans. As trying to regain my composure, my cell phone rang. It was my sister.

"Jaclynn," she said, "Sam is dead. He was stabbed to death."

"Wow. This is how she tells me?" I thought to myself, feeling a wave of shock ripple through my body, followed by a light sensation as if I might faint. "This is why people ask if you're sitting down," I also remember thinking to myself.

My sister went on to explain that Sam, her ex and the father of her three children, was involved in a late-night argument during which he was stabbed once in the shoulder. Though an ambulance had been called, an artery was struck, and he bled out on the kitchen floor before help could arrive.

"When did this happen?" I asked my sister.

"Late last night," she responded. "I've been trying to call you all day but I couldn't get my composure for long enough to make the call."

This was what I was feeling. I could feel her before the call. I could feel her anguish but I didn't have anything to attribute it to yet. I knew, without a doubt, that this was why I was emotionally distraught that day. However, when I tried to explain it to my boyfriend, he did not share the same sentiment. Some people just do not believe connections like this are possible.

On a lighter note, but in a similar manner, there's another way spirits occasionally make their presence known before sessions. Sometimes, I'll suddenly crave or desire something that the client or the spirit liked. The first time this happened, I kept obsessing about Baby's Breath flowers. This was odd because I'm not particularly fond of this type of flower. I searched several bodegas around my apartment until I found a bunch that looked healthy and pretty. Rushing back home, I placed the flowers in water and set them out on the coffee table just before my in-person session was about to begin.

My client arrived and settled onto the couch, stating, "It's funny," as she relaxed into the cushions. "Those are my mother's favorite flowers. I was hoping to hear from her today."

I've experienced similar manifestations in many various

forms. Once, I felt an absolute need to have a brand new notebook before starting a session. This was odd for me because I always finish my notebooks to the last page before moving on to a new one. And my current notebook was only half way used at the time. As I began the call with the client, she informed me that she had her new notebook open and was ready to go. I chuckled and asked if it was important for her to start with a new notebook.

"Oh, yes, most definitely," she explained. "A new experience always calls for a new notebook."

The interconnectedness we share on an etheric level never ceases to fascinate me.

REFLECTIONS ON THE EXPERIENCE OF CONNECTING

I want to share what the sensation of connecting with a spirit is like for me, which is a daunting task. I'm restricted to the use of human words and human senses to translate a process that is without a doubt not human. It's spiritual; from our consciousness even. And as a reminder, our spirits are shapeshifting, time-bending, realm surfers.

Connecting through a medium session is like having a memory or a thought in your head that doesn't feel like yours. Thinking about something is such a wildly magical experience. So much happens when we think–whether we're remembering, considering, or envisioning for the future. Just contemplate a thought. The deeper you go into that thought, or the more focused you are, the more you can perceive inside of it. You're not really hearing anything and you're not really seeing anything, however the thought is crystal clear and what you recall or imagine about these senses is equally as "perceivable." In some way, your consciousness is re-entering the scene.

A similar example would be a memory. We can recall the way someone sounded, how we felt, the colors of the scene, and what we were thinking inside the scene. If I ask you to imagine rubbing sandpaper across your jeans, you can see the jeans and you know what the sandpaper would feel like brushing across the fabric. None of this is actually happening, but you're in the scene through your thoughts. And so much can happen so fast. So many details are present and we get to revel in them for as long or as little time as we choose. You may have noticed the wash of your jeans, if you were sitting or standing, what color and grain the sandpaper was. You may have even seen yourself slightly ruin your jeans. And you were able to envision all of this in a millisecond. And this is what connecting is like for me. The full, vivid spectrum of the same sensations as having a memory enters my awareness. But the vision is not mine; it's different. It's somehow out of place and unfamiliar. It registers as slightly louder than my own thought.

Which is an important detail. When I work with clients, I always remind them that I'm not an authority on what's true or what's occurring on the other side. I can only share what I see, sense, and feel; then I always ask them to take my words to their heart center, tune in with their highest self, and ask if what I'm saying feels true or right for them. I think that no matter who you work with when it comes to connecting to the unseen, all of us should take our experiences from our sessions and the messages that come through during the sessions and run them through this process: take it to your heart's center and ask your highest self if it feels right and true. Keep the parts that resonate with you as truth, and simply discard the rest.

Incarnating as a human is a short, small process for a timeless soul manifesting in a physical body for a brief period of time. And when this time is over, the body disintegrates and the soul carries on. Having a medium session is an act of tuning in to the soul that's still very much alive and very much accessible. If we can wrap our heads around this concept even for a brief moment, we feel a soothing perspective of our lives. For a brief moment, we remember the magnitude of the soul and we realize that so much of what we worry about is insignificant and rather small in the grand scheme of our soul's journey.

It can be both frightening and a relief to consider the possibility that our souls have been here since the inception of energy and that they will likely carry on until the termination of the same energy – a concept that baffles science. We don't truly know how the first energy started. I'm talking about way back before the formation of the sky, the cosmos, the stars, the planet Earth – something sparked an initial creation and the truth is that we don't really know what or how. We have plenty of theories, but none of them are without flaw or proven to be completely true. Spirits have told me that we've all been around since this inception event and maybe even before. And that the other realms exist in a manner we can't truly comprehend with our human minds.

What's it like in the realm of spirits? Again, I can only share with you as I see it, but I would love to share this world I "see" with you. When someone initially dies, I have been unable to connect with their spirit for a period of three or four days following their earthly death. *Most* of the time. For every rule, there is almost always an exception.

I don't know exactly where they go, but when I am able to connect with them, I have a deep understanding that they've returned from somewhere magnificent. This place that they go is vast, wonderful, and extraordinarily healing for souls. It's not entirely accurate to refer to it as healing because that would imply that souls reach the other side in some way wounded. This visit to the magnificent place seems to be more about a reset through which the soul is reminded what it truly is.

There are physical, spiritual, mental, and emotional challenges that we all experience through our lifetimes as humans, and that spirits go to this place to free themselves of these experiences and to coalesce once again with the vibration of the spirit world. And my sense is that they have help. I experience this help as a light. It is vast, immeasurable even, and it has a personality. Intelligence, love, and support exist in the place of the light. When souls go to this light, they remember who and what they are.

I'll share one further reflection, for those questioning their own psychic connection. Before I realized I was a medium, I would often find myself daydreaming or overthinking seemingly random things about people I'd just met. These daydreams would go into exceptional depth and detail, and I would sometimes replay in my thoughts on repeat. At some point, I began to take greater notice of these thoughts. I started asking, "Why am I thinking about this so much? Why is this person taking over my thoughts? What is this phrase I keep repeating in my mind when I think about this person?"

I focused more on my thoughts as an observer, instead of a creator, and made attempts to categorize where the "thoughts" were coming from. It had never occurred to me that all of the thoughts that we experience are not necessarily generated from our own beingness. In fact, no one knows for certain where thoughts come from at all. As soon as I opened myself to the reality that thoughts could be coming from somewhere or someone else, things really started to click for me. This practice of categorization helped me more easily recognize spirit connections. Mediumship takes practice, learning by trial and error, and time. Every psychic that I know started their practice with a hunch that something different was going on for them and developed their skill over time.

GENETIC SIGNS, TESTING, & VISITATIONS

My journey into the realm of mediumship didn't begin with the polished skills I possess today, nor as described in my communications throughout the preceding chapters. So how did I become a communicator with the dead? As in, how did I know?

Becoming a psychic medium wasn't a sudden revelation or a single transformative moment in my life. It's not like I woke up one day with fully formed psychic abilities. Instead, it's been a gradual process and a journey that unfolded over time shaped by various experiences and encounters along the way. There wasn't a specific event that I can point to and say, "That's when I knew." It was more like a series of subtle nudges and expansive teachings from the universe, guiding me towards this path.

I've been sensitive to energies and have had intuitive insights from a young age. There were moments in my childhood when I felt like I was in tune with something beyond the physical realm, but I didn't fully understand what it was at my age. It wasn't until later in life, through a combination of introspection, spiritual exploration, and personal experiences, that I began to recognize and embrace my "connection abilities."

Many of us have experienced mysterious interventions from the spiritual realm at some point in our lives. It's curious how seldom we openly discuss these occurrences with others, yet studies reveal that a significant portion of the population confesses to having had inexplicable supernatural experiences. Fast-forwarding a bit, this speculation that many of us have had such encounters while few openly acknowledge them has been confirmed through my work as a medium. Over the course of my career, I've had the privilege of speaking about these profound encounters with nearly 2,000 clients, which underscores the widespread nature of such experiences.

There are distinctions between being psychic and being a medium, despite their close similarities. "Psi" originates from the Greek alphabet and is used by parapsychologists to denote various extraordinary phenomena. These phenomena encompass a wide range of abilities, including telepathy, precognition, clairvoyance, mediumship, telekinesis, psychokinesis, and beyond. When we refer to someone as psychic (Psi-chic), it could imply any of these abilities.

Mediumship, which happens to be the predominant psychic sense of my adulthood, involves facilitating communication between the living and the deceased, or the spirit world. This communication could include deceased relatives, spirit guides, soul teachers, and even our own higher selves. These entities of the unseen are vast in their appearance and are most likely being interpreted differently from one medium to the next. This is because despite our other worldly connection, mediums are still human beings having a human experience. Our understanding of the earth realm is based on our experience in this reality, which will influence the ways we interpret and describe what we are sensing from the other side.

A simple example of this is that a gardener might see an object and describe it as "vine-like." A cardiovascular surgeon might describe the same object as "veiny." And an avid hiker might hear both people's descriptions and argue that it seems more like a "trail system." Yet all three descriptions are about the exact same thing. Our experiences in this life as humans will impact our relationship to and descriptions of the unseen realms whether we realize it or not.

While all mediums possess psychic abilities, not all psychics are mediums. Simply put, mediums facilitate communication between living humans and the unseen world. Mediumship can be categorized based on the methods employed by mediums to establish their connection. This can involve various techniques such as seances, spirit channeling, ouija boards, or trance states.

We're all psychic at birth. Or we at least possess the biological ability to be psychic. Each of us is born with a row of light switches, with each switch representing a different innate psychic ability. For some, only one switch is flipped "on" at birth, while for others, all switches are "on." And perhaps many are born with all the switches turned down. The ability is there, it's just dormant. Regardless of how many are "on" at birth, as we socially develop with age, the majority of us begin to switch off these abilities.

Around the age of seven or eight-years-old, there's a notable shift in our cognitive development and self-awareness, marking the point when most children consciously start to dial down their natural psychic inclinations. This process can commence even earlier, possibly as early as age three. For me personally, this age from three to four-years-old was pivotal. Although I showed signs of being "different" even earlier on in my childhood.

Supernatural abilities are taboo in our society and are often discouraged in children. Children seeing spirits or predicting the future are all too often simply dismissed, leading to an unintentional suppression of innate psychic talents. If you don't use it, you lose it.

My childhood experiences reflected this. I don't remember these years of my life well, but my mom told me that she first noticed I was telepathic around eighteen-months-old. I started speaking at an early age, piecing together short phrases around nine-months-old. By eighteen-months, I could speak more freely and share my thoughts with her.

My mom is pretty laid back by nature. Nothing surprises her and there isn't a catastrophic event on the planet that could excite her. She's the prepared-for-anything type, unphased by alarming situations. So I know that I could have been an exceptionally offbeat child and my mother would not have registered it as "concerning" in any way. She and my father separated when I was nine-months-old, but maintained a cordial and supportive relationship for the most part.

One memory in particular stands out for my mom as it was the first time she knew my telepathy was more than just coincidence. She was looking through the cabinets in our kitchen trying to decide what to make for breakfast. I was playing on the floor, distracted by my toys. My mom decided she would make oatmeal and started to look for the pan to cook it in.

That's when I stared her directly in the eye and told her, "I don't want oatmeal."

From that point forward, my mother kept a journal of oddities that she noticed about me. To her credit, I never once remember her telling me not to talk about something or not to say something, regardless of how weird the things that I came to her with were. A lot of parents want to save their children from ridicule, so the process of suppression often begins from a place of love— a parent telling the child they have a silly imagination or laughing and brushing things off.

The first time I decidedly shut off a part of myself and my psychic connection was because of how a group of adults reacted to me. I was around three or four-years-old. Neither my mom nor I can remember my exact age, but we know for sure that I hadn't started school yet. Mom was having friends over for dinner and after they arrived and started adult talk, I got bored and went to my bedroom to play on my own. While in my room, a purple blob materialized and began talking to me, telling me that I could tie my shoe if I wanted to. It explained that it wasn't hard to do at all. This blob seemed completely solid to me, not a ghost-form nor a light-being, and was about the size of an armchair. The closest thing I could compare it to would be Slimer from the movie *Ghostbusters*, but purple and solid.

I distinctly remember putting on my shoe as the purple blob talked me through the way to work the laces. At some point, the blob intertwined with my energy and guided my hands at the parts where I was unsure. I remember watching the entanglement of our energies and the direction for my hands like it was yesterday. Within seconds, I had learned to tie my shoe. I came bolting from my room to the kitchen because I wanted to show my mom what I had learned.

"Mom! I can tie my shoe! I just learned. Watch!"

I was young enough that the adult audience of dinner guests was skeptical. I sat down with one shoe already on and tied, and the other in my hand. I put the second shoe on and proceeded to tie the laces without hesitation.

I looked up to see my mom pulling her chin back with a pursed smile and the most proud look in her eyes.

"Where did you learn that?" one of the guests asked?

"The purple man, " I answered excitedly.

"Is that a show?" the guest asked my mom.

"I don't think so," my mom said, starting to show some

confusion.

"What purple man?" the guest asked me.

"The one in my room. The blob. He's there now. He taught me," I responded adamantly.

This was a time before tablets and devices, when most families had one television that was in the family room only. We certainly did not have a television in my bedroom and the guests knew it. We were living below the poverty line and just didn't have the means for that kind of luxury. As the group slowly started to realize that I was serious, I saw their faces shift to looks of bewilderment and even slight disgust.

There was nothing said, just facial expressions made. And even at that age, I realized that I had said something "wrong," something that made me feel unlikeable. This uncomfortable emotion was such a contrast from the pride I had just felt from learning to tie my shoe with the visitor. It was a feeling of subtle shame. And I don't even think it was intended by the adults. But it shaped my psychic expression from that point forward, because it's human nature to want to be accepted by the group. Especially when we are young and vulnerable. I learned not to talk about what I learned from my visitors.

I don't know who or what the purple blob was. I remember it well and I recall having a sense that it was male, but a lot of non-physical beings are gender neutral. They have tendencies one way or the other, but they don't attach to the genders or sexes like we do on earth, and some of them don't have genders or sexes in their particular species or forms at all. I don't remember the purple blob visiting me ever again. It was a momentary teacher that perhaps I psychically cut off connection with after the feeling of exclusion from the adults.

I experienced numerous visits from various beings, ranging from human-like to distinctly alien forms, even encompassing ethereal light beings throughout my childhood. These encounters linger in my memories with remarkable clarity. Though for much of my life I attempted to dismiss them as imagination myself. Over time, I've come to understand that these memories are more than mere figments of imagination. They are real experiences that defy conventional explanation.

I don't recall a single visitation from non-human beings feeling scary. This distinction is important because I also remember abnormal visitations at school by human beings who would take me from class and put me through different sensory and intelligence testing. Recognizing that jumping from spirit or ultra-dimensional visitations to school testers is quite a different scenario altogether, both are worth noting because they fall into unusual memories I have from my childhood.

These humans that came to test me in elementary and middle school scared me. I sensed something nefarious, but I was too young to make anything of it. They were pulling other students from class for testing too, so it wasn't just me. Not like when non-human beings came to my home or to other locations to visit me. I was usually the only one to see them. What all of us tested students had in common was that we were in the top one to five percent of the grade in terms of our IQ scores.

There was one test that I received that my fellow top percentage students did not receive. It was a hearing test. I was called to the nurse's office for mandatory testing in the sixth grade, at age eleven. I was tested by two women who seemed nice enough but were dressed oddly in my opinion. Their outfits looked too formal for where I grew up in a small town in Texas. I was given headphones to put on and was then asked to face away from the women and raise my hand when I heard a beep. I followed instruction dutifully until the final test. I saw the woman press the button, but there was no beep, so I raised my hand anyway. I just figured the machine was not working right. The testing stopped abruptly and the second woman removed my headphones and asked me to turn around.

"Did you hear something the last time you raised your hand?" she asked me with clear hesitation.

"No," I said shyly. "But I saw her press the button so I raised my hand anyway."

The two women side-eyed each other.

"You saw her press the button?"

"Yes," I admitted.

"How?"

"In my mind," I started to tear up.

I was becoming scared now. I thought they were going to get on to me for lying. But I wasn't lying. I felt like I had done something very wrong from the way they were challenging me through their eyes and body language.

"You saw it in your mind?" she asked again.

"Yes," I said this time with a tear rolling down my cheek. I was ashamed and I didn't know why.

"Ok," she snapped her folder shut. "You passed your hearing test. You can go back to class."

Throughout the day, the lingering feeling that I was going to be in trouble clung to me like a shadow. Desperate for reassurance, I repeatedly asked my classmates about their hearing tests, only to find that none of them had undergone such examinations. There was one fellow classmate in particular, Andrew, that I thought for sure would have been tested. He and I were always competing for the highest grades and fastest test completions in Science and Math. But he kept telling me there was no hearing test. My inquiries persisted for several days after my own testing, but the answer was always the same. Andrew never got a hearing test.

At some point I let it go, and I didn't give it thought for over twenty-years, until a psychic researcher asked me if I ever had odd testing in elementary or middle school. It was only after this question that I reflected as an adult on the hearing test situation. I was facing a wall while being tested, but I clearly remember watching the woman at the machine. I was using my consciousness to observe outside of my body, something I now do regularly in my sessions as a medium. Something I probably did all the time as a young child, and also something I shut down that day of the testing.

I have speculated for years on why the school system seemed interested in extra-sensory perception, which is what psychic abilities are. I believe they are the result of an expanded nervous system perceiving beyond the standardly taught five senses. As I reflect on the involvement of the school system in assessing psychic abilities, it's become apparent that my speculations will remain just that–mere speculations. The precise reasons behind why some of us were singled out from class and subjected to strange testing by individuals dressed in professional attire, who were not regular staff members, eludes me. It is worth noting that this phenomenon appears to be widespread across the United States. My research has indicated that children whose IQs surpass the norm are often singled out for unconventional assessments.

Many of my psychic friends and colleagues report similar enhanced senses, like my hearing, which are referred to as "extrasensory" perception. These can be anything from the ability to hear electricity to the ability to see the flashes in LED light bulbs. LED bulb flashing is something I can perceive and it's maddening. You could imagine it as a subtle strobe light effect. If my husband and I are in a space with LED lighting after sunset, he knows I will be pressuring our departure soon (which I'm fully aware must sound rather bizarre to the average perceiver). We can't really come out and say, "Hey we need to leave now because you're totally unaware but these lights are flashing and Jackie can actually see it, even though you can't. So yeah, she gets a feeling like motion sickness and we need to go now."

Equally as troublesome for me and my heightened sense of hearing are these little devices that people plug into their outlets when they have pest problems. The devices create a supposedly indetectable sound that deters the pests. But I hear them loud and clear and the sound is incessant and unbearable. I will sneakily unplug them and set them on the floor if I'm stuck in a home where they're being used. One of my grandmothers has them and gets agitated with me because I take them out and then rarely remember to plug them back in.

Going back to the concept of innate or genetic signs, there were a few outlier memories that remain vivid and profound in my mind. I recall numerous instances not only of observing myself and my surroundings from an external vantage point, like I had during the hearing test, but also of experiencing another phenomenon: physical levitation. I did not experience levitation in the way you might imagine it from movies. It was not a slow lift to hovering slightly above the ground through forced concentrated effort, but instead more like a launch to ten feet above the ground, then a slow descent to a hover. I could only maintain this hover for a matter of seconds before I would release to the ground. Because of the height I would achieve, I could only do this type of levitation outside.

I recall doing this twice in my childhood. One could argue that perhaps I have fantasized memories of merely jumping higher than I thought I was. While that could be the case, I distinctly remember the fear of the descent and questioning my ability to keep myself from crashing down. Then I remember being overcome with a sense of relief that I did not make fast, hard contact with the Earth, but instead, came to a hover. It was as if I was an opposite magnetic force to the Earth, and we were repelling each other. This repulsion was keeping me afloat.

Both levitation and the ability to project our consciousness for astral observation seem to stem from a shared source within our consciousness, and they both require a similar kind of focused intention. On a more subtle level, this intention leads to the ability to astral project your consciousness beyond the confines of the body. On a more pronounced level, this same intention leads to the ability to temporarily break free of Earth's gravitational pull and physically levitate.

One vivid memory stands out from my early childhood—an encounter with human-like entities who engaged me in what appeared to be a simple ball game, but in truth, felt more like a test of some sort. I estimate that I was around three or four years old at the time, although in moments like these, it's challenging to pinpoint my exact age. I feel the same age in a lot of my memories as I am right now. It's as if I tap into a timeless aspect of myself. Re-entering memories is like accessing a part of ourselves that exists beyond the constraints of earthly time—an eternal essence that remains ageless and connected to higher realms of energy. Describing this experience of agelessness to someone who hasn't felt it themselves is difficult, but it's as if we possess "higher" selves, untethered by the limitations of physical matter, existing since the inception of energy itself.

In this memory, I found myself in the midst of a

strange ball test, conducted by beings whose appearance mirrored that of humans but had subtleties of extraterrestrial origin. These beings arrived in a disc-shaped craft that had a rolling ball on its underside, which could serve both as a means of landing and taking off. It was loud and clanky, as if it were scraped together–certainly not how one would envision advanced technology. Two beings emerged from the craft—an unmistakably male figure with a beard, and a female counterpart. While their resemblance to humans was striking, they were not human. They had a yellowish tint to them, which seemed to be coming from inside or emanating from beneath their "skin." As if their muscles and even perhaps their blood were a mustard yellow.

Facial hair was a feature exclusive to humans in my experience with other beings up to that point, making the male's beard stand out as a distinct oddity. This physical anomaly has remained etched in my memory, almost searing it into my brain.

It started outside in my backyard. They would send the ball in my direction and I would need to keep it from touching my house. I was told that my family would be injured if the ball touched my house. This rule was presented in the same manner as a child playing: don't step on the crack, or you'll break your mother's back. While it was only just a game, it ignited a deep anxiety that something bad would actually happen if I didn't perform.

As the game carried on, the complexity intensified. First, it was just don't let the ball touch the house. I would block the ball, then I would send the ball back. Then a rule was added that I couldn't let it bounce. I had to catch their throws then send the ball back. The throws became more and more difficult to reach but I stayed on task. The final rule was shared with me telepathically while the ball was in the air–I could not let the ball nor my feet if holding the ball touch the earth. So, I levitated. I shot myself up and I caught the ball in the air, then threw it back to them on my slow descent before hovering roughly an inch above the ground for several seconds. I remember seeing myself outlined in yellow light during my levitation. And then the pair left shortly after the last toss.

I felt anxious and fatigued after they left. Many of the "tests" throughout my childhood memories felt like I was being caught for something I needed to hide. And I often dreamt that I was running from someone, desperately trying to escape a life of enslavement. In fact, I still have troublesome dreams of frantically attempting to escape capture.

I have replayed this ball game memory over and over in my mind, probably hundreds of times. I have created excuses for it, tried to convince myself that it was a dream, and even attempted to brush it off as my own overactive imagination. I've played with the notion that it was ET contact. I've researched types of UFOs and found nothing like what I remember. Through my research, I've read about others who have had similar experiences.

I even met one young man who had almost the exact same ball test at around the same age, also from off-planet beings. Ultimately, though, these are simply the facts of what I remember. And to remain true to myself, I cannot state anything further about this incident. This is what I remember, exactly as I remember it.

PROPHETIC DREAMS

Prophetic dreaming was another ability that I presented from a young age. This happened less often than my telepathic communication or my interactions with beings, but the dreams were certainly just as unusual. My mom said that she never paid much mind to my uncanny dreams when I was a young child, because my dreamtime predictions would play out to be close to reality but not exactly accurate. I would wake up and share the dreams with my mom or my sister and something similar to what I had seen would occur–usually on the same day. It wouldn't be an exact translation, but close enough to be memorable.

I don't remember any of these dreams from when I was young. I've only learned about them from my mom. The first dream that I remember happened when I was a freshman in high school. I was in a deep-sleep and I recall coming in and out of this deep-sleep state three times, with a sudden jolt each time that I woke. I looked over at my alarm clock and saw that it was the exact same minute in time, all three wakings. This was a really odd feeling for me to go from such an alert awake state to such a deep sleep multiple times in the same minute. When I woke up that morning, I told my mom and sister about what had happened and that it was weird because it was exactly 1:11a.m. every time I woke up. We were in the car on the way to school, and within seconds of sharing this experience with them, we heard a radio announcement that three high school students had been shot and killed shortly after 1:00 a.m.

I think both the timing of the radio announcement and the thought of the shootings occurring three times back-to-back caused all of us to have a strong emotional reaction. It was probably the intensity of our shock that has led to me remembering this dreamtime experience over any of the others I had when I was young.

As I matured into my late teens and early twenties, the dreams became more intense and more accurate. One prophetic dream in particular really broke my heart. This dream was close enough to give me an alarm, but not accurate enough for me to truly do anything with the information coming through.

I was working as a server at a restaurant while I was in college. My shifts were part-time and mostly on the weekends. My manager at the restaurant had two jobs; the one at the restaurant and another as a paramedic. One night I had an intense dream that my manager was out in the middle of a field doing chest compressions and CPR on someone.

When I arrived at work the following morning, I told him about my odd dream. It had been a while since I had one of these dreams and my goal in sharing was really to call out how weird it was that I was dreaming of him. I shared that I figured it was probably just because I knew of his other job, and was perhaps thinking about work the next day when I went to sleep.

That same day, two men came into the restaurant on motorcycles. They were lovely guests, probably in their late fifties or early sixties, enjoyed a nice lunch overlooking the lake at the restaurant, and then drove off on their motorcycles. The restaurant was about thirty-minutes from any kind of major town. I think that they rode out just to take in the beauty of the countryside and eat a nice country meal. Within minutes of their departure, I saw my manager bolting out of the kitchen through the side door.

This wasn't unusual as the restaurant was part of a lake resort destination and little things happened often that required immediate attention. About an hour later, he came in sweaty and white as a ghost. He sat down at the booth nearest to the kitchen. I could sense that something was terribly wrong. I felt the strongest desire to just ignore his obvious distress. And I did for a while. But eventually, I had to cross his path to get to my tables.

I walked by him and asked, almost dutifully, "Are you okay?"

"No," he told me, "I'm not."

"Those two men that left were in an accident. One of them was on the concrete driveway and his front wheel accidentally swerved off and he veered into the field. When he tried to come back onto the driveway, there was an elevation in the cement and his tire slammed into the side of it. His friend said that he flew forward into his handlebars, fell sideways onto the ground, grabbed his chest, and told his friend to call 911. I heard the dispatch because I sometimes stay tuned into my radio and realized that it was for two men just outside of the restaurant. I ran out to find him lying in the field beside the driveway and proceeded to do CPR and anything I could to save his life. He died under my hands."

Even to this day, thinking about this event brings up a deep, unsettling sadness within me. Of course there's no way that I could have known who my dream was for or what it was about. I could never have predicted that something like this would happen to the man on the motorcycle. I try to reconcile it within myself by considering that he wasn't even going that fast. His friend said that they were driving less than twenty miles per hour. The driver was just looking around at the view and lost focus when he swerved. A simple, small mistake. But something inside me still feels heartbroken about it. They were such kind and happy gentlemen, just out enjoying their days.

I don't always understand the ways of the spirit world. I don't understand why it was the motorcycle driver's time or why I was given that dream. People often ask me if I feel it's a curse to have these abilities. I don't think so, but it does hurt sometimes. I have been hard on myself in feeling that if I was "tuned in" just a little differently, maybe I would have deciphered that dream in a better way and been able to save this man. But I'm not tuned in differently and I don't know why—some things are clear from the spirit world and some messages are not.

I was actually fired from that job within a few weeks following the accident. I don't think my manager ever recovered from his experience. He definitely never looked at me the same. And while he tried to be cordial, I could tell that he felt guarded. I even sensed that he was worried around me. I've often asked myself if he thinks that something about me made the accident happen. Does he think that I brought it to be?

Superstitions are not uncommon for people who don't understand psychic connection. People sometimes think that mediums have much more power than we actually do. That we have an upperhand in the spirit world and can bend the future to our will, perhaps through spells or some kind of magic. Whatever it is they think we're doing, it would definitely have to be connected to the darkness.

This concept makes me giggle inside. No one has less desire to engage with dark forces than myself. I have my own life that I'm trying to live from a place of love and service, and my own family and endeavors that I'm trying to create the most out of my life for. I just picture someone believing that I go home at night and pull out my Ouija board and start my spell-casting...when in all reality, I'm picking up toys and loading the dishwasher before bed.

One of the most intense dreams I ever had occurred in September of 2019. I was an established medium at this point, roughly ten years into my career. What I had wasn't entirely a dream, it felt more like being in a deep meditation, and then snapping out of it to find myself awake. I had made a solid mental connection to distinct visions, feelings, and even what registered for me as a warning.

I was living in New York City at the time. My dream-state visions were of martial law in the city, long lines for food, military operations in the street, as well as highly-planned, organized military led projects throughout the city. When our dreams or visions come from Spirit, they have a certain tone or pitch. They somehow feel different than our own thoughts and even our own imagination. That's how I knew that this was not the standard dream. It was much more crisp and had a tone of caution.

My best explanation of how dreams from spirit feel different from other dreams is to consider how our ears can perceive different voices. The sensing and receiving that we do as spiritual beings makes it possible to differentiate between sources, as they have the equivalent of different tones. The same way that you would know the difference in your mother's voice versus your spouse's voice, you can train yourself to recognize the guidance and who it's from. These visions about New York City were clearly from my higher guidance.

I will elaborate on this much more in the chapter about my guides. But ultimately, I believe our individual souls, our guides, source energy, spirit, and all deceased loved ones are one and the same. They just show up differently so that we can identify them and begin to have a relationship with them. I don't mean to confuse anyone when I interchange these terms in my descriptions. I think the way they show up is important, but I also trace them all back to the same source of energy.

So because of the clarity of tone from my guidance, I trusted this dream on a deeper level than I ever had before. I made immediate and drastic changes in my life. I had been living in New York City for over a decade at this point. I was well-established with a clientele that I adored, and my medium practice was expanding exponentially and globally.

I rented a beautiful apartment one block from Central Park, and maintained a schedule and lifestyle that I cherished. I also had expendable income, something that took me seven years to create in such an expensive city. But I made up my mind that morning that I was going to leave. I wanted out. The tone of this dream vision was impactful. It was exact, it had a precision unlike any of the others before it.

Within weeks of the dream vision, I broke the lease on my apartment, which is almost unheard of in New York City. But I found a loophole and I got myself out of it. I sold off most of what I owned, boxed up the rest and shipped it through a company to an undisclosed address in Dallas, TX. The shipping company gave me ten days to report my address, as that was how long it would take the driver to make his drop-off route and get to Dallas. I rented a car, loaded my cat, and drove back to my hometown of Denton, which is just outside of Dallas. I had a dog at the time that a very generous ex-boyfriend agreed to fly down to Dallas after I had arrived.

Within two days of my arrival in the Dallas area, I found a gorgeous apartment on the outskirts of the city limits. If I walked out my apartment door and turned right, I would enter Dallas. To my left were open fields of countryside, filled with walking trails and many miles until the next small country town. I was living outside of Dallas less than a few months, when the word of an outbreak took to the news. Within weeks, almost the entire world went into lockdown as we were informed that this was the safest measure to keep a life threatening virus from causing unnecessary deaths.

In the middle of the crisis, there were troops on the street in New York City. It did become a sort of military operation in that there were naval ships brought in and parked at the piers around the island of Manhattan, along with overflow beds in a makeshift hospital setting. There were more sick people than the hospitals could accommodate. There were also semi-trucks parked outside of hospitals, which were guarded by uniformed security staff, to allegedly temporarily store dead bodies. Outside of the grocery stores, you could see long lines for food because the stores limited the number of customers allowed in at one time to prevent contamination.

The city put in place strict curfews and limited individuals on their rights to interact with each other or businesses. Even the number of people allowed in a group was monitored while outside. No one was allowed to eat inside a restaurant and eventually the restaurants in New York City set up services outside on the street for customers.

Prior to my departure, I was trying to warn my medium clients of what I had seen in my dream vision. I kept trying to convince them that something was coming. I think the majority of my clients probably thought that

I'd finally lost it, as I was also simultaneously getting pretty deep into my esoteric research. But when it comes to my connection messages, when I know, I know. And this was something I knew without a shadow of a doubt. Something was coming and it didn't feel good.

I wanted to help my clients by warning them, but I was inadvertently pushing them away. We were told as a population that these lockdowns would last for two weeks, but it became obvious quickly that this would not be the case at all. This change in our lives was going to be much longer term, as were all of the new social rules and restrictions.

I started receiving messages from the clients around week six of the lockdowns. A few of them admitted that they thought I was nuts at the time, but could now see how spot on my predictions were. Two of them asked me if I thought the restrictions would lift soon. We were at around week twelve at that time. I told them no, I did not believe so, and that I saw New York City creating a type of travel pass at some point. Those two clients actually moved out of the city in the weeks following our conversations too. And as predicted, NYC did put vaccine measures in place; vaccine cards became a requirement for residents to patronize local businesses.

I believe my guides knew that I would not have fared well in New York City under those conditions. Instead, I was in a state where the mask mandate was removed fairly quickly and the residents of the state were granted the right to go out anytime much earlier than most other states in the country. It also helped that I lived close to nature walks, where I could get out with my dog and enjoy my feet on the earth. There's no political agenda behind sharing this. I had many friends who stayed in New York City and they did just fine. They figured out a way to navigate the circumstance in a manner that worked for them. But I believe my spirit guides intervened because they knew that this would have crushed my soul to live in such an environment.

I don't like to feel restricted from my time in nature. And I also don't like waiting in lines. I avoid public events because I don't want to wait in line for food nor to use the bathroom. I rarely, if ever, attend concerts or large conferences–and bars are a disaster scenario for me. I couldn't imagine a life where my time outside of my house was monitored or one where I waited to enter a grocery store, though I know much of the world lived like this for many months.

I also sensed the subtle influence of my late grandfather, his voice echoing in the recesses of my mind in the weeks preceding my departure, gently urging, "Pack your bags, baby girl. Head home." Interestingly, shortly after relocating, I crossed paths with my now-husband, Neil —a pairing that also seemed guided by my grandfather. But the intricacies of this serendipitous encounter will unfold in the chapters to come.

It's now common for vivid dream visions to frequent my nights, reminiscent of the one preceding my departure from the busy streets of New York City. I typically only share these nocturnal glimpses into the unknown with my husband, Neil. Our life decisions often stem from the insights gleaned from these ethereal journeys. With time, I've become better and better at discerning their prophetic undertones. Unlike the vague and fuzzy dream preceding the motorcycle accident, these visions are strikingly clear and specific. Whether it's the result of my extensive psychic training or the deep bond forged with my spirit guides–or a bit of both–I can't say for certain. Nonetheless, I'm immensely grateful for this channel through which the spirit world communicates with me.

While I think our dreams come from many different sources, I believe dream visions are our spirit or our spirit guides asking us to pay attention and to make change. In order to do so, they often intensify the emotional response we feel or the severity of what's occurring in the dream. This is to ensure they get our attention. They need to disturb our comfort state so we'll take heed.

We can acknowledge the message from our spirit and our spirit guides and thank them for reaching us in the dream vision, then ask that they tone down the emotional intensity. If you begin to let them know that you received the message (loud and clear) and that you are willing to evaluate your life and make changes accordingly, the next dream will come through with less intention to be emotionally disturbing and more focus on the clarity of imaging.

When I started integrating this practice into my dream response, I noticed that the dream severity toned down, and that I could decipher the messages a lot more clearly because I was focused on what I was "seeing" instead of what I was "feeling" in response.

* * *

The other sources of dreams that I've experienced are:

• Visitations from our relatives

• Messages from our guides - both in the form of warnings and affirmations

•Reactions to content consumed in the short period before going to sleep created by the brain

• Soul school time, when we often see ourselves in a classroom or absolute black space receiving messages from teacher

• Astral projection, when we are outside of the body and sometimes outside of time-space

• Interactions with nefarious, non-human beings (these are typically exceptionally disturbing)

• Interactions with angel-like light beings (these are typically glorious and deliver beautiful messages)

• Absolute gibberish and indecipherable unfoldings which I believe are a product of EMF overload on the brain

I share these many sources of dreams for others to begin to consider their own dreamtime experiences. In addition to my tip about reducing their intensity, I also recommend that you start to distinguish from where your dreams may be originating. Most people have never even considered that our dreams might come to us from different sources. We naively just sort of "lump" them all together and thereby miss out on significant learning opportunities.

You can begin to recognize the "tone" of your dreams,

much like I did. And when we recognize the tone, we can understand the source. Just like associating a voice with a human, we can associate a dream tone with the origin of the message.

It will help to know when you're receiving guidance, when a dream is just a jumbled mess from brain processing, when a teacher is showing up in the astral to work with you on something, and so on. Start by working to categorize the variety of dreams you are experiencing and where you believe they are coming from.

TIMELINE SCANS

From a young age, whenever I engaged with individuals, particularly after locking eyes with them, a cascade of clear and precise visions would flood my mind. These scans did not happen all the time, and certainly did not occur for every person I made eye contact with.

The visions disclosed troubled moments from their lives with startling clarity, revealing not only their age but also the circumstances surrounding them and the emotional toll it exacted. It felt as though a timeline of their existence stretched out before me as an invisible holograph. I could then see bright spots on the timeline where significant events occurred. If I focused on the spot, the entirety of the event would unfold in my awareness. All of this would happen within a millisecond.

These bright spot events weren't the conventional milestones society typically deems significant—graduations, weddings, career advancements. Instead, they were painful junctures that reshaped the very essence of the individual, leaving a sort of distortion in their vibrational resonance.

I call this ability "Timeline Scanning." I could see

moments when traumas or painful experiences occurred that altered the person's unique vibratory signature. The result of this trauma was that they would lose a little bit of their direct connection to Spirit, as if their new, distorted vibration signature (which carried the frequency of the trauma) was no longer a match for conjunction with higher realms. They were, in terms, more heavily bound to earth. Simply put: our painful experiences, if left unhealed, can separate us from our highest connection to Spirit. And I could see these moments for some people.

I believe we're all born with a unique vibration energy that is pure, unadulterated, and connected to Spirit. It has been my own observation with my son, Moss, that children seem to shift back and forth from this realm to others quite easily. It is as if their consciousness is sometimes here in the present with us on earth, and at other times adrift in communion with the unseen. They are literally part here and part "out there," deeply connected. There is something about our original, unique vibratory state that finds ease in establishing connection to the unseen. As we age and develop, accumulating all varieties of experiences, we become more and more bound to earth—no longer traversing multiple realms with such ease.

Upon reflection, it is blatantly obvious to me that this ability is not typical to the human mental process. If I had known what to look for, this would have been an obvious indication of my "psi" or supernatural attunement being beyond standard range. But the thing about the way we're all wired is that we don't know that we're having different experiences until we start to evaluate our thoughts. We don't realize that we might be thinking or experience mental processing differently than our peers until we actually stop and think about our thinking. Which was something I was not even remotely interested in doing, let alone capable of doing, until I was well into my twenties. I don't know if this was a product of my upbringing or perhaps because I started using drugs and alcohol at the age of twelve and continued into my early twenties. Substances were a definite inhibitor of self-reflection in my case.

As far as I knew, everyone was having these kinds of intuitive insights about people when they met. I didn't know that I was different because my thoughts had just always been the way that they were. For me, I didn't know that this Timeline Scan was actually an accurate form of psychic insight. I thought this was just something that we as humans did, and that we didn't talk about because we didn't really need to.

When we understand someone on a deeper level, we can treat them with a deeper level of compassion. I love this forthcoming example, because this was a real event from my life that showed me the other side of this ability. I got to experience what it would be like to not have the Timeline Scan ability. I inherited a dog through my marriage. When he was around twelve-years-old, he started slowing down significantly, only waking to nudge me in the leg roughly two-hours before his feeding time, which he then continued to do endlessly until I fed him. He had stopped hearing well, and often lagged behind on walks that we would take as a family with our other, much younger dog.

One day, I took the senior dog to the vet for a check up and to evaluate a lump I found on his hind leg. We learned that the lump was cancerous and that because of his age and his intolerance to sedation or anesthesia, there was not much the vet could offer in terms of treatment. He was essentially sent home to pass naturally with instruction and support for keeping him comfortable and as pain free as possible until the end.

After knowing what was going on inside his body, I no longer got annoyed when he nudged me for two-hours before feeding time. I would go find him when it was time for potty walks instead of yelling his name, because I knew he couldn't hear me well. I also started taking him on separate, shorter walks so he could go back home and rest instead of fatiguing, and I found myself all around cuddling him and loving on him more.

I had an epiphany shortly after the vet visit. He was the same dog, with the same behavior, in the same environment. But I was treating him differently because I had an understanding of his inner world and the reality of his situation. And this is what Timeline Scans did for me. They allowed me a certain level of grace, patience, and compassion for an individual because I could see what had hurt them and what was still affecting them.

Interestingly, I didn't see the shadow side of people in my Timeline Scans when I was a child. Perhaps this is because children haven't developed their own shadow selves yet, so they don't recognize them in others. But I became aware as an adult that people hang on to these painful and difficult things that happen to them throughout their lives and in doing so, they inadvertently impair their emotional processing abilities. A common result of this clinging to the pain is difficulty in relationships and failed attempts to create their highest and best lives.

We don't always do this at the level of awareness, but we all make decisions about how we move forward from these Points in our lives. There is not necessarily a conscious decision that has been made, but we are different.

I have worked with a client in my adult years, through my medium practice, whose situation is a perfect example of the subconscious processing we have after an event when decisions were clearly made by her mind and body without any effort of logical thought. She was roughly four-years-old when this event happened. She was at a baseball game with her parents. I had prompted her towards this age and a sporting event in our session together because I saw clearly in my Timeline Scan that something had happened and it had permanently broken her trust towards males in her life. After my prompting, she knew exactly what it was.

When the client was four-years-old, she was busy paying attention to the baseball game and was not fully aware of her surroundings for a brief period of time. When she was finished watching that part of the baseball game, she reached up to grab her father's hand. After they locked hands, she looked up to his face. She realized immediately that it was not her father. It was the father of another kid at the game. And while she told me that he was a nice man who seemed like an understanding parent that was completely aware of the nature of her mistake.

He was in no way threatening whatsoever. But she was petrified. She started screaming and crying hysterically, desperately searching for her biological parents.

I asked her if she could identify what was upsetting about this moment to her child self. She explained to me that she realized how easily she could be fooled. How you can think you know who someone is, but you better not trust it. And she had carried that fear with her ever since, though she didn't realize the full extent of the belief until our session together.

We worked together on her subtle energy processing so that she could return to the vibration of who she was before she assumed the false belief system of never trusting someone's character and always watching out so she wouldn't be fooled. While this was a lighthearted event, it was life changing for her and affected her belief systems well into her thirties. Considering the innocence of her situation, one could imagine the impact a more serious, more traumatic, or more nefarious experience would have on an individual. You may even be able to recognize your own painful memories. They stay with us, standing out in our memories amongst a sea of events we simply don't remember at all.

I've learned through my medium practice that some people want to go back and evaluate these points of their lives. There is a process to travel deep inside with energy work and meditative exercises to induce vibrational healing, and thereby move forward differently. More aligned with our original vibrational signature. And there are some other people who simply don't want to change. They hang on to their traumas and often allow them to be an excuse as to why they never spiritually grow, nor are they able to do the things that they want to do. This is the shadow self.

My Timeline Scans are a reminder of the interconnectedness of humanity, the shared experiences that bind us together. I came to understand that this unique ability is not a mere coincidence, but a major part of who I am. And while this ability was spontaneous for me in my childhood, I've taken great interest in strengthening this avenue for psychic connection within myself.

Throughout my life, there have been other one-off occurrences of things happening that were definitely psychic in nature. But telepathy, prophetic dreams, and Timeline Scans seem to be my dominant forms of natural ability. These were the switches that were "on" for me at the time of my birth. They are the ones that I turned off at some point in my childhood and have actively worked to flip back on in my adult journey.

If any part of my ability to perform Timeline Scans resonates with you and you're eager to enhance your abilities, I wholeheartedly recommend reading *The Emotion Code* by Dr. Bradley Nelson. Its chapters are filled with insights and understanding of how specific vibrations become imprinted in the body, their profound impact on our well-being, and practical methods to release and restore them both for yourself and others.

I often joke that *The Emotion Code* is the book I would have penned myself if it hadn't already graced the shelves. It's truly a treasure trove of wisdom and knowledge. Even if you don't aspire to develop the ability to psychically "view timelines", Dr. Nelson equips you with invaluable techniques, such as muscle testing, to pinpoint the age of emotional distortions and their impact. He also offers guidance on using a strong magnet to facilitate a profound energetic reset, which helps restore you or your client's original and unique vibrational state.

So, whether you're seeking to deepen your understanding of energy healing or unlock untapped potential within yourself, *The Emotion Code* can be a wonderful tool on your path to self-discovery and transformation.

You might be beginning to wonder, "What about mediumship? Isn't that the subject of this book?" Indeed, the ability to communicate with the deceased is at the heart of my journey, but the ability to communicate with the dead was not present in my childhood whatsoever. The great revelation of my ability to talk to the dead surfaced in my early twenties.

SENSING THE DEAD

In my early twenties, my dormant psychic abilities unexpectedly evolved into something remarkable —mediumship. It seemed to emerge almost by happenstance, a connection I hadn't actively pursued or anticipated.

I left Denton, Texas for graduate school in Australia when I was twenty-years-old, fresh from completing my Bachelor's degree at the University of North Texas. I graduated from high school at seventeen. Academia was easy for me, but moreover, I did not like school. I struggled socially and never felt like I fit in or had great friendships. My solution was to just get it over with as quickly as possible.

I had landed a job in a real estate office near Sydney to financially support myself while pursuing my graduate studies full-time. My days were a whirlwind of academic endeavors and work responsibilities. Occasionally, when all of the agents at the office were occupied, I found myself tasked with showing potential buyers through listings that were for sale on behalf of the busy agents.

One cloudy day, I went to meet a couple that were interested in a house coming up for auction the following weekend. Australia is unlike the United States in that listing a house for auction typically brings the highest value and many people chose this route of sale to drive competition. Agents will show the house for a few weeks leading up to the auction date, when all interested parties will come to the property to bid. This house was odd to me as it had been completely renovated but there were no other interested parties that I could recall before this couple I was showing through.

As I drove my car into the driveway, an ominous sensation gripped my gut. Suspecting it was just the cloudy, dreary day, I dismissed the feeling and carried on. I stepped out, determined to dispel the shadows creeping into my mind, and approached the door with a mixture of apprehension and curiosity.

I unlocked the door to see a beautiful scene of pristine cleanliness and dazzling brightness. The renovation was stunning. But beneath the surface of this immaculate interior, an unsettling vibe lingered. Ignoring the subtle sense, I attributed my unease to the unfamiliarity of the surroundings.

As I walked through the property, I began to notice a vague tingling feeling creeping up the right side of my face. It was a subtle but undeniable sensation. I walked through the living room towards an adjacent side room, which was the only carpeted space in the house. I approached the entryway with the intention of flipping the light switch inside the room. However, as I extended my hand to do so, I came to an abrupt halt. It was as though an invisible force prevented me from crossing the threshold. In an instant, a vivid image flashed through my mind—a dark-haired woman with a frantic expression. Simultaneously, I experienced a sensation akin to a physical blow striking the right side of my body.

I froze.

I tried to compose myself and calm what I thought was my imagination. "What an odd place to go with your thoughts, Jackie," I said to myself.

Despite my efforts, I found myself completely unable to enter the room. It was as if an invisible barrier held me back, intensifying the discomfort coursing through me. I could liken the sensation to being lightly tased in the heart, though I've never had this done to me. That's just what I suspect it would feel like. It was a feeling so profound that it triggered an instinctual fear of danger. This wasn't merely a matter of discomfort; it felt as though my very survival was at stake, sending shivers down my spine and setting my nerves on edge.

I went outside to wait in my car until the couple arrived. I wanted to be comforted. I dialed my then-boyfriend's number to talk to him about the peculiar experience. I was in a particularly stressful phase of my graduate studies and I was working a lot. I told my boyfriend that I thought I was probably getting overly stressed and not in a good mental place. He was actually the reason that I was able to find a job in Australia. He had been in real estate for decades and knew the owners of my office well.

"Wait, are you at the house on Groves Street?" he asked me.

"Yeah, the renovated one."

Then he said casually, the way only the most laid-back Australian can, "Ah yeah the bloke clubbed his girlfriend to death in the side room there. It was a garage they converted. That's why it's all renovated and there's carpet in there. They couldn't get the blood off the floor totally."

I was young, twenty or maybe twenty-one. I couldn't remember ever being in a place where I knew there was a murder. I was processing so deeply that I barely responded to him. "This must be how we feel when we stand in the spot where truly bad things have happened", I thought to myself, assuming all humans could feel what I felt and it was only unique because it was my first time to feel it.

As I sat there, absorbing the information, my mind raced with a flurry of thoughts and emotions. At such a tender age, the concept of confronting the aftermath of a violent crime was entirely foreign to me. I found myself struggling with a multitude of questions, each more perplexing than the last: "How could a seemingly ordinary house harbor such dark secrets? Was I overreacting to a mere sensation, or had I truly stumbled upon something sinister? I saw her. I felt things in my body." These facts gnawed at the corners of my consciousness, leaving me feeling emotionally unsettled.

The couple arrived within moments and I did my best to snap myself out of my darkened mental state. It was my job to show them through the property, and I didn't want to emit any kind of weirdness myself. I wanted to be professional and figured everyone but I knew about the history of the house. I took them through politely, fielding the questions I knew the answers to, while they walked around the interior. They had saved the side room for last. As we approached the threshold to enter, I braced for their response to the energy.

But they didn't stop. The women went right in, flicked on the light, walked to the center of the room, turned around in a circle a few times, and made some comment that I can't remember anymore. But I know for certain that it had nothing to do with the way the room felt or the fact that a woman was brutally murdered in the exact place she was standing. A woman whose blood was under her feet, beneath the circles she was turning.

I felt sick. Not because this woman didn't care. For all I know, she truly had no idea, just like me fifteen minutes before. I felt sick because this was the moment I could no longer deny that I was truly wired differently. This was the moment I knew deep inside that I was reaching other realms; or better yet, they were reaching me.

While sensing this murder was undeniably a pivotal moment for me, it didn't immediately lead to my acceptance of being a medium, despite the profound impact. Looking back, I realize it should have been a catalyst for acknowledging my mediumship abilities.

Instead, I spent many years after that vision of the woman (and many more spirits to come), grappling with doubt and uncertainty about my experiences. Each spirit encounter and revelation added another layer to my understanding, gradually leading me toward acceptance of my mediumistic abilities.

Following my tour of this property, I couldn't resist the urge to verify what I had seen. I turned to my boyfriend for any insight he might have on the couple. He mentioned they were of Lebanese descent, a detail that statistically would have aligned with the image I had seen of the dark-haired woman. But there was always a chance that it didn't. The boyfriend I'm referring to at this time was also of Lebanese descent and his mother, who was born in Lebanon, had golden hair and light eyes.

I refrained from going any deeper into my research. I'm confident that if I had been determined enough, I could have uncovered police reports or even an obituary. However, I was plagued by a sense of shame and found the prospect of continuing my investigation into the murder too unsettling and morbid.

From that point forward during my time at the real estate job, whenever I learned of a house where someone had passed away, my curiosity led me to explore further. Whether the death was natural or unnatural, I felt compelled to immerse myself in the space. There was an inner guidance pushing me to learn more. I would visit these specific properties as soon as I learned of a death. In most cases, I could only sense the lingering energy, a subtle reminder of the lives once lived within the walls. I did not get the same intense visions as I had in the remodeled house.

One notable exception was an abandoned insane asylum, where I encountered the presence of an older woman. My boyfriend drove me out to the property late one night as he had once felt a presence there himself. He knew I was trying to make sense of my experiences and we both wondered if I would feel it too. Though this woman did not seem to have passed through violence, her troubled and confused spirit left a lasting impression on me. She was disheveled and I saw details of her appearance. She was thin, with unkempt, gray hair. She was trying to talk to me through her eyes, though I was not receiving any direct messages. But I could feel her frustration; a sense of being trapped.

These experiences were not undertaken for amusement or boasting. Instead, they served as a personal quest for validation. I was driven by a need to prove, or disprove, the reality of my encounters. But it's impossible for me to corroborate my experiences if I don't have someone to validate with proof or verification of the people who were there and have passed. Even to this day, I don't know if there was actually a woman that died in the asylum.

During my time in Australia, from the age of twenty until I was twenty-three, I never once identified as a psychic medium. Despite the undeniable accuracy of my connections, I viewed them simply as inexplicable experiences rather than a defining aspect of my identity. It wasn't until later, upon reflection, that I would recognize the significance of these encounters.

Plus I was in a relationship with a boyfriend who, in hindsight, exhibited some mediumistic traits himself. It's interesting how two psychic individuals in a relationship can remain oblivious to the fact that they might both exist beyond the "norm". Instead of acknowledging our unusual experiences, they can go completely unnoticed, especially when neither person perceives their connection as out of the ordinary. As I've discussed in various sections of this book, this lack of awareness can be a significant barrier to recognizing and embracing our true psychic connection capabilities.

We fail to identify anything as out of the ordinary simply because we've never known any other reality, at least not consciously. Our experiences are confined to our own thoughts and sensory perspective, and without exposure to alternative perspectives, we remain oblivious to the concept that we're atypical. Simply put, we don't always recognize our differences because we've never known it any other way.

OTHER PLANS

When I was twenty-three years old, I left Australia. I had completed graduate school and stayed for an additional year of work experience in Sydney. I would need to apply for Australian Residency if I wished to stay any longer. I wanted to travel the world. I had been in school since I was five-years-old and working since I was fifteen. I didn't feel ready to make that kind of decision—whether or not I wanted to become a resident of Australia. Though in my heart, I didn't think that I would be happy there long-term. It was far from home, my family and friends rarely made the trip to visit, and my boyfriend and I had broken up. I didn't have any reason to stay, but I didn't have a different, better plan either.

There was no strong pull to return home to Denton, and living in Sydney had shown me that life without a car was not only possible, but in many ways was advantageous. I never had to worry about parking, public transportation was easy, and if I did want a car, I could rent one for a short term, which is much cheaper than buying a car and all the associated expenses that come with it.

I was young and carefree. I decided to travel for a bit and figure out what came next for me. I was renting a furnished place in Australia and I didn't have many possessions. It was easy for me to wind my luggage down to one checked piece and one carry-on with a few weeks of preparation. I put some of my things on eBay and shipped a couple boxes back to Texas. I wanted to travel light and set a personal goal to only book one way tickets until I decided where I would stop for the next phase of my life.

I traveled through Thailand for six-weeks, then booked a one way ticket to Israel, which was not a country I'd ever considered visiting. But there were a lot of Israelis traveling in Thailand, and they convinced me to check it out. I planned to visit for two-weeks to sight see the Holy sites, as well as any part of the country I could make it to during that time. I ended up staying for seven months. I met a foreign correspondent for a major broadcasting company during my short visit who was looking for a babysitter for his children in exchange for learning about journalism from him. My Master's Degree was in International Communication and this seemed like a no-brainer opportunity to witness real life journalism while also staying in a country that I happened to have grown fond of.

I had a wonderful experience, both in the country and during my time with this family. I decided that I would like to stay in Israel for a while. The correspondent that I was babysitting for was going to try to help me get the documents in place that I needed to legally work in Israel, so we put a plan into play. I started taking free language classes, called ULPAN, in order to both navigate the culture better and make more friends. I was surprised by how easy my whole situation had come together. And even more so, that I ended up somewhere that I had never even considered with potential to land a job in my exact field of study. Until things took a sharp turn. Spirit definitely had other plans for me.

I decided to take a weekend trip to Cyprus to explore nearby cultures and learn more of the regional histories. Cyprus was stunning and the trip was everything I hoped for. I met lovely people there and had the perfect tourist experience. Before my return flight to Israel, some locals that I had befriended took me out for Zivania, a traditional Cypriot drink. I was slightly buzzed and ready to relax on the short flight back. Once the plane had landed, I deboarded and headed to customs to re-enter the country through Ben Gurion airport.

I handed my passport to the station clerk. She held it on her side of the partition and began asking me a series of questions.

"Who are your relatives here? Where were you for Seder? Are you taking Hebrew classes? Do you have a boyfriend?"

I was doing my best to answer politely and honestly. I was still slightly buzzed from the Zivania and while I thought the questions were odd, I wasn't overthinking it.

Next thing I know, the customs clerk pulls out a stamp and slams it across the page of my passport, multiple times. "Wait here," she ordered.

Within moments, two heavily armed gentlemen made their way towards me. One of them gave a stern order in Hebrew.

"What?" I asked, really confused at this point.

"Come with us now," he said, this time in english.

I was baffled. Shocked. Beyond confused.

"NOW," he repeated.

I stepped towards them. The customs clerk handed my passport to the other gentleman, who then collected my bag. Then they escorted me through the terminal into a side room before sending me through two additional layers of secured doors.

I was asking questions. "What is going on? What have I done? Where are you taking me? Can I make a phone call?"

No one said a word to me. Not the two gentlemen, nor the three agents we met in the secured room. It was as if I was completely mute. Not a single person acknowledged my voice. They began disassembling my luggage and everything inside it. As they were picking apart my belongings, a fourth person entered the room, this time a woman.

"Come with me," she said.

I was taken into another side room where I was given a thorough body search. I did not have to take my clothes off, but I may as well have. My buzz was essentially gone and the violation of it all began to sink in. It was unjust. Cruel almost, the way I was being treated. All of my things scattered out on a table with multiple people rummaging through them, a body search, being completely ignored—and with no explanation. But demanding answers was of no use. I was unworthy of eye contact with these people, let alone a response.

They repacked my bag and I was taken out of the secure room, back into the airport terminal, where the two armed gentlemen handed me off to airport staff. The woman they passed me off to walked me to a row of chairs and sat me down. She took a seat beside me. "My handler," I thought to myself.

"Do you speak English?" I asked.

She looked at me with disgust. "Of course I do," she scoffed.

"Where am I going? And where is my passport?"

"I don't know," she said snarkily, though I sensed she was being honest. "And you'll get your passport back when you get there," she finished.

We waited in the chairs for about an hour. It must have been well after midnight at this point, but the airport was still bustling and alive. Two different men approached us and there was an exchange between them and my handler in Hebrew. Then I was passed over to the men, as was my baggage.

They escorted me to a side door, where we exited onto the tarmacs. I was handcuffed, loaded in the back of a white van, and driven to a location less than two minutes away.

"Where am I going?" I asked the men in the van.

"We are holding you overnight," one of them answered.

"Holding me?!? For what??" I gasped.

"Until your flight," he answered.

"My flight to where?" I demanded.

"How should I know," he laughed. "You are not my responsibility. At least not that part."

They unloaded me from the van and removed my handcuffs. We walked into a small concrete building with several cell-like rooms and one observation station.

"You can go in here to sleep," the man told me. "This is not jail, so if you need something, you can just ask."

I was led into a room with four bunk-beds, two of which were taken by other women. I was given my bag, but still did not know where my passport went. I climbed onto a lower bunk and laid flat on my back, in total disbelief of every detail of my life at that moment. I must have laid there for several hours, listening to one of the women in the room snoring. I remember thinking how relaxed she must have been to have been deeply enough asleep to be snoring. I was almost jealous. I was riddled with anxiety, unanswered questions, and the intense fear of the unknown–like where I was being flown to, and when.

I got up and knocked on the cell door. One of the men

from the van came to the door.

"Can I come out?" I asked. "You said this isn't jail and I'd really like to come out of this room please."

The door swung open.

"Do you need something?" he asked me.

"Yeah, actually. Am I allowed to smoke?" I was scared to ask but there's never been a more relevant time in my life to admit that I truly had nothing to lose by asking.

"Yes. Come with me. You want coffee?" he asked.

For some reason his question was the point when I started crying. It was the first moment of kindness or consideration anyone had shown me since I entered customs.

"Yes, please," I responded, gratefully.

He walked me outside and set me down at a picnic table. I had cigarettes in my bag but he insisted that I take one of his. He lit it for me and told me to wait, that he'd be back with warm coffee.

He returned a few minutes later with my coffee and another guard. The three of us sat at the picnic table in the early hours of the morning, just before dawn.

"Why am I here?" I asked them.

"You are not welcome in our country," one of the guards explained.

"What. Why?" I was extremely confused.

"I don't know," he responded, with a hint of teasing.

"So what happens now?"

"We don't usually know that either," he admitted.

"What about the other women in the cell?"

"Now that I do know, because they told me. They are being sent back to Romania."

"Why? Did they just fly in too?"

"No. They were caught. Prostitution."

"Why Romania?" I asked.

"Because that's where they're from."

"Am I going back to the US? Or Australia?"

"I told you that I don't know, Sherlock."

We actually all laughed. It was the first bit of lightheartedness I'd felt in a while.

"What did you do?" The other guard asked me.

"Scout's honor I have no idea why I'm here right now," I held my hand up.

"Scout's honor?" he asked.

"Yeah, it just means I'm really telling the truth. I'm not sure why I'm here or what's going to happen to me."

I explained my entire story to them, including the attempt to earn a work permit and my trip to Cyprus. I told them how much I was enjoying the country and was trying to be respectful, studying Hebrew to learn to communicate in the local language.

"You study Hebrew, eh. You want to marry me?" one of them asked, clearly teasing. "Then you can stay no problem. We can make you Jewish in no time. I know a rabbi."

I laughed and said that at this point, I'd do anything to just understand what was going on. We continued chatting, probably going through half a dozen cigarettes each over the next couple hours. Right at the break of dawn, a white cargo van drove back over to the pod on the tarmac. Two armed men came out and showed a passport to the guards.

"Alright, Sherlock. You're up," he said. "Good luck."

At least they have my passport, I thought to myself. I was handcuffed and loaded into the back of the van, alongside my small bag. Everything else that I owned was in my room in Jerusalem. We began driving down the tarmac, passing the door to the airport that I had come out of the night before.

The drivers were speaking casually to each other in Russian. Neither was paying much mind to me in the back seat. It was just another day at work for them.

"Wait, where are we going?" I asked.

"To your plane," the driver snapped.

"I don't even understand what is going on," I started to
cry again. "My plane to where?" I pleaded.

"You are not welcome in my country," the passenger
responded, with a thick Russian accent.

I am ashamed to confess what I blurted out next.
Exhausted, humiliated, and feeling like I had been
pushed around and treated unfairly, I was fed up
with all the secrecy surrounding my fate. The constant
mistreatment from everyone except the guards made me
feel subhuman. At that moment, I lost control and lashed
out.

"Well, judging by your accent, this isn't your country.
And you all just steal everyone's land anyway, claiming
territory that never has been and never will be truly
yours. So sell your stupid little self your bullshit lies all
you want but I'm not taking it."

The driver looked over to the passenger with a smirk.
They both chuckled.

"And can you please take off my handcuffs? This is
ridiculous."

"I will take them off," he responded, "But you better not go
anywhere."

Where would I possibly "go" I thought to myself? Am I
going to hurl myself out of this van on the tarmac, then
attempt to outrun any one who chased me in the middle
of a big, open airport runway? These people are strapped

with AK-47s. What a delirious statement.

"I won't," I confirmed.

We came to a stop beside an airplane with a portable ladder rolled up to the back entrance.

"Let's go," the passenger said to me. "And don't try anything."

I climbed from the back of the van out onto the tarmac and was then escorted up the ladder to the plane, one man in front of me, and one man behind me. Both were within inches of my body. As I climbed the stairs to the plane, I could see that it was a fully boarded passenger plane. The men stayed in formation inside the plane too, walking me to my seat towards the front. As we approached the single empty seat on the plane, the man in front handed my passport to the stewardess.

I was released to take my seat and buckle in. The two men left through the back of the plane. Shortly after the back door closed, the flight attendant approached me.

"Are you okay?" she asked me, tenderly.

"No." I snapped at her. I was raw and feeling like the fact that I was not okay should have been obvious. I responded as if all of this had been her fault. "Can you just tell me where we're flying to?" I found myself holding back tears again.

"First flight to Cyprus this morning," she told me.

I slept most of the flight back to Cyprus. Over the course of the night, my cell phone had lost its battery charge.

I didn't have a converter with me, as it had slipped my mind whilst packing for the initial trip out that Cyprus would have different outlets than Israel. I had three changes of clothes, very little cash left, and the only credit card I had on me was a debit card linked to an Israeli bank account that I had set up to deposit my babysitting money. I had closed my Australian cards before leaving the country, in the slight chance that I did not return from my journey to find myself traveling around the world. In my closet in my room in Jerusalem was a debit card linked to my US bank account, where I kept $1,000 as emergency backup money.

As I approached the counter of customs, it crossed my mind that I could potentially be denied entry in Cyprus as well. There was no way they would miss the page full of "Entry Denied" stamps on my passport from the night before at the Israeli customs. The woman slammed my passport at least a dozen times.

And if I was denied entry, then what? Would I be sent back to Israel? I kept thinking about the guard telling me that they ship you back to wherever you came from. My stomach sank as I came closer and closer to my turn at the customs line. I just imagined an endless disaster of looping flights back and forth between Israel and Cyprus. I didn't have a phone. I didn't have clean clothes. I could not imagine going back into a holding cell again.

It was my turn to approach the desk. I slid my passport across to the customs agent and waited in dread. He opened the passport and began to flip through. He came to the blacked-out page where the Israeli customs woman had cut loose with her stamp.

He raised an eyebrow and looked at me.

I shrugged, defeated.

He looked back down at my passport and then to me again. He smiled.

I raised my eyebrows and waited.

Then he dipped his head towards the exit, signifying my permission to enter, stamped my passport, and handed it back.

Silence hung between us as I accepted my passport and proceeded through the exit, no words ever exchanged. At that moment, I realized something unexpected. Although my life had just been flipped upside down, I was a free woman. It was a sensation unlike any I had ever experienced, a surge of liberation that would alter the course of my life in profound ways over the ensuing months.

Exiting through the airport gate, I stepped into the refreshing embrace of the open air. There were no guards, no handcuffs, and no waiting out a mystery judgment. I found myself without plans, money, a phone, or many possessions to my name. Without a job or any affiliations to bolster my ego's sense of identity, I was unburdened by obligations. With no one to answer to, I was faced with the stark reality of unadulterated freedom—a concept that, paradoxically, can be profoundly daunting.

THE TREE IN THAILAND

E verything that I had built my identity upon had gone. Up to this point in my life, I was a daughter, a student, a graduate student, a foreigner seeking work experience. I could explain what I was doing with myself if someone had asked. But suddenly I had no answer. There was a weird difference to me between traveling to find myself and traveling because my plan had been pulled out from under me. I could now no longer explain what I was doing, which caused me to lose a sense of who I was. When our external securities like our job, our homes, our relationships, or our goals are stripped out, knowing who we are is wildly elusive. I didn't see it coming.

I entered a dark, contemplative period of uncertainty and self-doubt. Up until this point I had made bold, brave decisions in my life. I dared to take chances on and for myself. Moving to Australia was one. Traveling alone around the world was another. Even my nonchalant attitude about the education system throughout high school was radical. Most other teenagers were enmeshed in social activities and their popularity status. I just wanted out. I felt there were bigger things in life than this silly system of academia. I only went to graduate school because my grandfather had pointed out to me that I would still finish at the same time as my "friends," graduating at twenty-one alongside my peers who would also be completing undergraduate at that age. I had agreed to do it, so long as I went to a really fun university. This is why I ended up in Sydney.

I realized that I had built my identity on just that— bucking the system. Making hard things easy. Moving to bold places. Venturing out alone. I feel that the ego compels us to be greater; to reach for big goals. In my case, my ego was also distracting me from a vast, inner world that I had neglected for most of my life.

As I took a few days to reflect and compose myself in Cyprus, I kept thinking about a moment I experienced in Thailand, just before flying to Israel. I still think about it to this very day, actually. I was standing beneath a tree, having just walked through the local market on the island of Kho Phi Phi. It was sunny, the water was beautiful, and I had spent the day with lovely friends that I met on the island. We finished a delectable lunch from the market and were heading to the beach for a beer and to watch the sun set.

And there I was, unhappy. I felt uncomfortable. I wasn't satisfied, which was upsetting me even more because I recognized that I was living in paradise by most standards. I distinctly remember looking up a small hill at a beautiful tree and asking myself, "When am I ever going to find happiness?"

I stood, silently, in deep contemplation. The warmth of

the sunlight on my face. Time seemed to slow and a silence came over me.

"You don't *find* happiness," a voice came through. "Happiness is a choice. And you can choose it anytime."

This was probably the first time I made direct contact with my guides in my adulthood, though I would not realize that for a few more years.

"I don't know how," I answered.

"It's easy," the voice gently responded. "We can show you the way if you'll allow our help."

"Well. I've got no better plan," I thought to myself, though the same entity certainly heard too.

Then I snapped out of my trance-like moment and rejoined the conversation with my friends. But the message stuck with me. It was something I would replay over and over in my mind for many months after.

This experience is of utmost importance. I had committed to accepting help. Even though it wasn't clear to me at that point in time. I believe that my spirit knew I wanted to end up somewhere that would be spiritually and emotionally fulfilling. I wanted to do work that would make a positive impact. And more than anything, I wanted to put an end to a lifelong discomfort I had learned to cope with. So I had agreed to receive help finding this place from the loving unseen, whether I realized it or not.

And we always get what we ask for. Israel was not this

place for me.

I stayed in Cyprus for two weeks, hanging out with an editing crew that a journalist contact had put me in touch with. One of them generously allowed me to crash at his place while I attempted to unravel the mystery of my entry mishap in Israel. Despite frustrating phone calls to the US embassy and later the Israeli consulate, the only certainty I had was that I was banned from re-entering the country for five years. The reason remained elusive. It wasn't until approximately a year later, during a visit to the Israeli consulate in New York City, that I discovered the shocking truth: I had been deported under suspicion of espionage.

This still cracks me up. It's just far-fetched and absurd. I never learned anything further about my deportation, like why I was suspected as a spy. From Cyprus, where I was able to straighten out my finances and organize the shipping of my possessions from Jerusalem to Texas, I decided to continue on with my travels. Aside from the back and forth from Cyprus, I was still technically living out my plan of one way flights around the globe for a year.

I kept returning to this moment in Thailand when I felt confused. For a long time, I questioned if the tree had spoken to me. I've always had a natural reverence for nature, and I genuinely thought it was possible that I had tapped into something sacred on the island. But an event a few years in the future would explain the voice I heard.

After several more weeks of travel throughout Europe, I made a decision to try and land a job in New York City. My time in Europe was difficult. I was beginning to tire of travel, being alone, and struggling with my identity issues. I still did not have a plan or a way to talk about myself to others. I found myself feeling embarrassed when I met people who asked the standard, ego-centric questions about my origins, my work, etc. In response, I started avoiding people altogether, unless necessary to interact. I was also drinking a lot and even partaking in local treats in cities like Amsterdam. The tree that I spoke with in Thailand was still connecting with me, gently reminding me that happiness was already available. I couldn't make sense of it and my attempts to just "be happy" were not working, so I would numb out with substances and more travel.

I arrived in NYC in the fall of 2009. The U.S. was in the middle of a recession following the housing crash and financial crisis of 2008. I had never even visited NYC and I knew nothing about finding a job. These are little facts that I'm blown away by in retrospect. The naivety of youth is a form of courage in and of itself.

I applied to two-hundred and fifty jobs, received five responses for interviews, and was given one offer for a receptionist position, which I gladly accepted. I found an apartment with a roommate that was a five-minute walk from a yoga studio that accepted donations for attendance. I was starting to put together some semblance of a structured life.

RECOGNIZING THE GUIDES

Within weeks of starting my new job in NYC, I realized that I was going to need to get my act together in a big way. The city has a competitive environment, attracting individuals of exceptional caliber to its workforce. I didn't want to stay at my receptionist job forever.

I stopped drinking. It only took a handful of nights out on the town for me to realize how quickly I could get caught up in the nightlife of the city and lose sight of my goal to do meaningful work. I couldn't shake the thought that I hadn't gone to graduate school for nothing. I felt that there were endless opportunities available to me in this massive city, I just needed to be ready to seize an opportunity when I got it.

I went to the donation based yoga studio regularly. Probably five times a week. It kept me occupied, distracted me from going out to bars, and was getting me into great shape. Plus I knew I could go to a class no matter how little money I had available. I wasn't making much in my receptionist role and my rent was absurd.

The more I went to yoga, the more I started to connect to the guidance I felt from the tree. But I no longer had the urge to numb it out. Instead, I started to feel interested in the guidance. What was it? Who was it? Was it me? Dedicated to a life of sobriety and living without much expendable income, I shifted my focus towards trying to understand my inner world better.

It was easy to do since I spent most of my time at a low pressure job, the yoga studio, or my apartment. I wasn't going out anymore and I cooked at home most of the time to save money. I started shedding years of attachment to fitting in socially. Not necessarily the need to fit in, but all the concern I had over the fact that I didn't. In a city as densely populated as Manhattan, it was easy to become invisible.

Within a few months, I was able to secure a much higher paying job at a management consulting firm, where I would stay for the next three years. With my higher paying salary, I decided that I wanted to become a certified yoga teacher and enrolled in a 200-hour teacher training. This is where things really took off for me on the psychic front.

Not only was I being exposed to the teachings of the East, but I was also really focusing on my body, my breath, and my relationship to myself. Sobriety was affecting my brain health in both a challenging and beautiful way. I could no longer run from my discomfort or block it out with substances, and was instead learning how to simply be with it.

There was one exercise during the teacher training when things started to click for me. We were asked to sit face to face with one of our fellow students and stare into each other's eyes for one minute without talking. It was an awkward task, although I really liked the group of students in the training. I was paired with a woman I didn't know that well.

In that moment, I found myself seated, heart wide open, embracing myself in a manner I hadn't dared in all my years as an adult, with the newfound clarity born of sobriety. I readied myself for the exercise as the teacher signaled to begin. I suppressed a childlike urge to giggle and lifted my gaze from the floor to meet my partner's eyes. And then, the culmination of a lifetime's experiences converged into a single, unbroken flow of direct connection.

My awareness was flooded with visions. I saw three babies, dead, all shown to me by a young male spirit. I heard a voice from the unseen say, "It's not your fault." I saw scenes of my yoga partner crying on the floor in the depths of the night. There were calls to mom and the replaying of a single song, over and over. I saw her hand turning a round knob on the stereo to make it louder. I recalled the time she arrived at training reeking of alcohol. "She was grieving," I heard from the unseen. I loved her. Because I felt it all too.

This moment was everything combined: my Timeline Scans, my medium connections, the loving instruction from the guidance at the tree—my abilities had all coalesced into this one solitary experience.

And it happened in a flash. I sat in awe, tears welling in my eyes, for at least another forty seconds. When the timer stopped, we were asked to share what we had experienced with the group. I couldn't. I lied and talked about myself, saying I was preoccupied with my own thoughts for the minute. It was a half-truth.

After class that day, I pulled the woman aside. There was no way I could let her go without telling her what I'd seen and finding out if any of it made sense to her. She shared with me that it all made sense, and that it was all accurate. She had just experienced her third miscarriage and was not doing well. She was drinking a lot and blamed herself for not being able to keep the baby alive.

I kept in touch with this woman for many years following our teacher training together. She had a son within a year of that exercise. She shared with me that when he started talking, he once said to her, "I had to wait a long time to come to you mommy. I had to try a lot."

This event was a turning point for me. It was the point when I realized that I could willingly make psychic connections. Because I had sat down to look into her eyes with the intention of gathering information from the unseen. It worked, and it was accurate. I didn't know what to do with it yet, but that answer was coming very soon.

After graduating from my teacher training, my yoga school offered me a part time role as an instructor, leading early morning classes before transitioning to my office job for the day. I taught three 5:00 a.m. classes a week for several months, finishing at the yoga studio by 6:15 a.m. to then shower, dress, and head to my day job.

I was less than six-months into my yoga teaching when another psychic breakthrough happened in class. There was a new man in my class. Every time I circled by him while instructing, I had an intense feeling that I should pay particular attention. I was making sure to check on him often and adjust his postures more than I would the average student. I wasn't attracted to him; it was something beyond that. I was receiving guidance from the same source I first met in Thailand, and it was pushing me to grant this student more of my awareness.

I was reluctant. I felt the push to go near him, but I also felt odd and in disbelief that this was a good idea. Regardless, I did listen to the guidance that I was hearing and followed the instruction to take special care of him. When we took the final pose of class, called savasana, I followed this inner urge again to go and lay my hands on his arms. It is typical for an instructor to offer an adjustment in this pose. As I knelt down to the floor, I felt driven to place my hands on his forearms. As I got close, I saw a horrific scar up one of his arms.

Time slowed. I began questioning my own sanity. "What are you doing, Jackie?" But I persisted, and as my hands rested on the scars of his wrist, I followed a guided nudge to whisper, "You're safe now."

I slowly stood up, turned from the student, and lightly walked away. Inside, all I could think was, "What the actual eff was that, Jackie?"

I was beyond uncomfortable. It was clear to me that this student had at one point in his life attempted suicide. It wasn't a small scar–it was like a lightning bolt shooting down and out over the multiple areas where he had butchered his arm. This realization of his attempt to take his life led me to question if I had made a misjudgment or been misguided. I felt like my behavior was invasive and it was disheartening to consider that I had been *guided* to do this. What if I misunderstood? What if that guidance was just my own impulse? I don't want to cross the lines of someone else's privacy or ever feel that I'm invading their energy space. Why would the guidance have me do this? The one minute exercise a few months earlier felt different because it was voluntary. But I had done this to him, and without his consent.

After class, I waited at the desk as I always did to wish the students well and thank them for our time together. The man who I had adjusted hung around at the desk for longer than the average student. He told me that it was a really special class for him and he was grateful that he had shown up that day. He continued to come to my classes for the next few weeks, hanging around a little longer each time after class and chatting.

One day after class, he asked me if I remembered the time that I had touched his arms. I admitted that I did and I was about to apologize. But before I could, he instead told me of his suicide attempt and admitted that for some reason, when I touched his arms and whispered to him that he was safe now, he felt that he had finally outgrown the period of life where he questioned if it was worth living. He told me that he'd never spoken about this before but for some reason he knew he was beyond this season or this phase of life. He shared that the experience in class that morning was moving and he couldn't thank me enough.

What he didn't know at that time was the impact that encounter had on me. To gain clarity on whether or not I'd done the right thing that day, I booked a session with my mediumship teacher. Her name was Florenza, and she was someone I was connected to by my acupuncturist. Florenza resided in Hawaii. I wanted to ask her if I had done something wrong or if I was in fact being misguided. We had an hour-long session together where we talked about many things, but I couldn't get up the nerve to admit to her what I had done. I was experiencing a lot of shame after this incident. I kept trying to build up the courage to tell Florenza about it and ask her what I should do. The call was coming to an end and I had failed to bring it up.

Right before we hung up, she said to me, "You know Jackie, those voices you hear – the one you heard in yoga? They're beautiful, they're right, and they're pure. And it's important that you listen to them and that you try to trust. They are coming from the highest place with the intention of the highest good for all."

I broke down in tears and finally admitted to Florenza what had happened and how insecure and wrong I felt about the whole thing. And how deeply embarrassed I was that I was hiding it. She assured me that I could trust the voice when it sounded or felt like that and that I might not understand why, but that I should try to have the courage to lovingly follow through.

Because the student had been open and vulnerable with me, I actually opened up to him about what that incident had been for me. I told him that I was realizing that I am a medium and that I get visions or connections for other people and that I believe they're coming from a place of the highest good for all. I asked him if he would be open to meeting with me and talking with me more. He said he couldn't be more honored. Within a few weeks, we had a session that ended up being deeply accurate and profoundly healing–for both of us, I'm certain. There was definitely a reason why Spirit was trying to reach him through me.

He became my first official mediumship client. And from this session with him, my professional mediumship business grew. He referred me to some of his closest friends in Brooklyn, who then referred me to their friends, and so on and so on. I even had a session with his mother. Over time, his mother and I became friends and even went to yoga together a few times. They're a beautiful family, and through a mediumship session with the mom, I was able to connect to his grandmother who had passed. She was a real rebel who still inspires me to this day. I sometimes wonder if it was his grandmother coming through that day in the yoga class, but I could never say for sure.

I began moonlighting as a psychic medium on evenings and weekends. My medium practice was steadily growing, mainly through word of mouth. With the additional income from my medium sessions and yoga teaching, I found myself able to shift from full-time office work to part-time contract jobs. As my practice took off, I was able to space out my contract jobs more and more. Even still, I wasn't clear that I would become a psychic medium as my full-time career. I cherished the breaks from the corporate world. I couldn't ignore the increasing disparity between the boundless energy of my medium work and that of the stark, cold, and structured corporate environment. But New York City is an expensive place, so I continued to accept contract offers at companies I found interesting, especially if I believed they were doing good for the world.

I found myself in a weird dilemma attempting to manage who knew about my psychic abilities. It was like navigating a maze of secrecy and paranoia. If a new company I was interviewing with did a simple Google search of my name, they would find my website and know about my mediumship practice. I didn't think they would want a candidate like me in the kind of analytical roles I was taking.

Interestingly, as I reflect on my current practice, many of my clients come from executive and entrepreneurial backgrounds. It's a fascinating evolution, considering my earlier struggles with secrecy. Today, I offer a long-term program tailored specifically for the business world, recognizing the increasing alignment between spirituality and professional careers. In a business context, I help clients acknowledge the profound significance of their spiritual pursuits and the invaluable guidance awaiting us from the realms beyond, should we choose to embrace it.

The pressure of maintaining a facade in the corporate world eventually reached a breaking point for me. I accepted that not only could I not manage who knew what about me, but that I didn't want to worry about it anymore. The aforementioned contrast between the polished corporate environment and the reality of my psychic experiences became increasingly unbearable.

I was in a contract role for a company in New York City's Chelsea neighborhood. It was a stressful day at the office. I was working in operations for a rapidly-growing startup in a high pressure environment. On this crisp fall day, I was feeling particularly suffocated by the weight of it all while simultaneously being distracted by my personal struggles with emotionally taxing medium sessions the night before. I made an uncharacteristic decision. I abandoned the confines of the office and ventured out for a solitary walk along the piers at the Hudson River. It was a departure from my usual unbroken routine, a spontaneous act driven by an urgent need for clarity and alone time.

I wasn't a big fan of workday breaks as I've always found it easier to just keep my focus on my role and responsibilities than to segment the focus with a break. I prefer to stay locked in concentration, then stop at the end of the day and shift entirely out of work mode until the next day.

But I was nearing a breakdown. And I felt a strong pull to the water. It wasn't a pull actually, it was like a compulsion. I had to follow it. I'm also not a fan of cold weather, especially when there's any kind of precipitation outside. Going to the water on a cool fall day was completely out of character for me.

But I went. And I found myself arguing internally on my walk over: "Why'd you make me this way? Why can't you be normal? This is a great freaking job with a phenomenal company–what is WRONG with you?"

I felt out of place and confused. And I was getting angry. I could tell myself to practice gratitude and be logical all I wanted, but it was no use. Because my brain was saying one thing—to settle down and stay put—but my body was experiencing something totally different. My body was telling me to follow a different path.

"What do you want from me?" I asked, desperately.

"Who are you talking to?" I heard back.

It was such a simple question. Like, the most basic. But it was a pivot point for me. Because in that exact moment, I realized that I fully believed that I was talking *to* something. I realized that there was another side to the conversation–it wasn't only me receiving, but that I could ask for more. There was something else, others, and they were talking to me and helping me through an active conversation.

I'd never considered that this was a two way conversation between me and others, despite fully recognizing a guidance from a force greater than myself. Something about this conversation made the connection personal. There were identities behind the guidance. And there were several of them. I couldn't make out an exact number at the time, but I sensed a small group.

I started to cry. I sat down on the ground. Not a bench. The ground. This is an important detail that I'm sharing because it's a common reaction. People tell me that when their big breakthroughs happen, their legs give out from under them. They crave the support of the earth and they just drop. And that was my experience. I wanted to be cradled by the stability of the earth touching every part of my body possible.

Then I gave in. Or gave up. I'm not sure. But I surrendered to a truth that I'd know for quite some time. That there is an invisible world and this world is trying to work with me. And even more specifically, there are unique, identifiable personalities in this unseen world that want to be a part of my life. I freely opened up dialogue with them, no longer resisting or denying my connection.

"What am I supposed to do?" I begged.

"You can trust us. We are here to help."

"This doesn't feel helpful. It feels freaking disruptive and isolating," I angrily responded.

"You have a gift. And we want you to use it to help others."

"Cool story, brah," I laughed. "But are you going to pay my bills?"

"Yes. You are going to be taken care of."

"But what if I hurt someone?" That was and still is one of my greatest fears.

"You may hurt others. But only because you cannot control how messages are received," they explained. "The truth can hurt in your dimension. But we work only from a place of the highest love. And you can make that your intention too. We promise."

"This is nuts," I thought to myself. Because I felt, sensed, and heard their connection in a clear, undoubtable way. And I felt my own soul expanding. Despite the oddness of it all, I felt more myself than ever. "This is nuts and I'm on board," I repeated, in disbelief.

"Alright then, let's do this," I agreed.

Something about it all—even though I didn't know what "it all" was—was so thrilling to me. It felt like the bravest, truest thing I'd ever decided. It was similar to my feeling in Cyprus, except this time it was made by choice.

And despite a still small, nagging resistance from my logical self, I walked back to the office and quit my job on the spot. It was a high paying contract and I was on the hook to pay back a signing bonus. But I just had a feeling that this was real and that I would be guided.

The guides that I had connected with on the river also told me that my life would feel uneasy and that I would constantly struggle internally if I didn't learn to trust my connection ability and trust that it would be useful for others. While my logical self was leaning one way, my spiritual self won this decision. I sensed that they were behind my experience at the Ben Gurion airport in Israel, they were the voice I heard at the tree in Thailand and in so many of my medium sessions, and they were the ones rewiring my energetic body to no longer match the vibe of the professional career environment in New York City.

If I had to pinpoint one emotion that has most fueled my journey toward becoming a medium, it would undoubtedly be discomfort. If I could offer a piece of advice to fellow spiritual seekers or those who suspect they might have mediumistic abilities, it would be this: embrace that discomfort and turn inward. Listen to the whispers of your innermost self. It's through this introspection that the path to connection becomes clearer and more profound. It's the easy way. The shortcut. Right into the pain.

On this day at the piers, the guides were mere voices that I was receiving telepathically. Over the coming months, they would begin to appear as hovering lights, perceivable only through my mind's eye, which we often refer to as the third eye. With time, I would uncover their true physical form. And it was not what I expected.

WHAT ARE MY GUIDES

Explaining my beliefs about the origin and nature of my abilities takes things to a new level of strange for most people. In addition to the genetic predispositions I've discussed at length and the visitations from my childhood, I believe there's an additional explanation. Simply put, I believe that before I was human, I existed as a different life form—something more akin to an alien. In my previous existence, I inhabited a different realm, perhaps even a separate universe, where communication was exclusively through telepathy. We had the ability to manifest our needs directly from the metaphysical to the physical realm using the power of our minds. We wanted for nothing and anything was possible, because we worked with our powers of creation all the time. Meaning anything we could imagine, we could bring to being.

Through deep, transcendental meditations, I've seen this place as a purple-blue planet. I am totally gray, much smaller, and do not have body hair. There are hundreds of thousands of us and we all look the exact same. There is no physical sign of gender, though we have two genders. We all wear gray, fitted bodysuits that feel like velvet to put on and though we are each individual, separate beings, there is a sense of oneness. A harmony, you could call it, amongst us—because we can all experience the emotions of the others around us. The purpose of this life is community. There's no striving for greatness or acquisition of the material, because we are all capable of creating whatever we choose in any given moment. Imagine the world if we all had machines in our homes that could generate anything we desired or give access to any endeavor including experiences like travel and entertainment.

The energy that we embody in physical form, and that we return to between lives in physical forms, maintains a memory. I entered as a human on the planet Earth with a memory of the form of communication from my gray-being life. This memory includes the ability to communicate through telepathy and the ability to engage with another person's experiences as if they are my own through my Timeline Scans. They don't happen all the time and I don't have Timeline Scans with everyone, but they do seem to be guided by some sense of purpose.

My abilities as a medium are tied to a relationship I have with five other beings that I believe visit me from the world I lived in as a gray-being. They don't just visit, they seem to also help me. I call them my guides–The Five. It's important to share that so far, I've encountered eight guides. There are the five guides that made themselves known as the voices on the pier by the Hudson River, though I did not know it was five of them at the time. They are also the source of the guidance I received near the tree in Thailand.

Then there is one set of twins that saved me in Spain and one guide that came through clearly for me in one of the darkest moments of my life. I will share about each of my eight guides in depth.

The Five first made themselves known through telepathic thought, as described through my experience by the tree in Thailand. I "heard" something, but I couldn't distinguish where it came from or whether or not it was simply my own intuition. My connection to them became a primer for more telepathic connection to other spirits. I think they were literally wiring my nervous system receptors for better mediumship.

Following my experience at the Chelsea Piers, I continued to hear from these guides at random intervals over the next few years. It was the same type of clear telepathic communication, and always when I was by bodies of water. One conversation in particular happened while I was on a walk by the ocean in Hawaii on vacation in my late twenties. Just a fun detail: I was listening to music on my iPhone on shuffle and Maroon Five's "Come Away to the Water" came on at random during this beach walk. It was actually there in Hawaii that I understood exactly how many guides there were. Prior to this encounter, I had sensed that there were multiple voices but couldn't make out how many.

I wanted to know more about who or what these guides could be. I wanted to know why and how our conversations worked. What were the voices? They must have some form of identification if I could sense that there were five of them. I couldn't be the first person on the planet to have this kind of experience. Surely there were teachings somewhere that would help me learn and understand more.

I would eventually ask every teacher I had. None of them could answer my questions, nor point me in the right direction to understand my guides. I went to a lot of expensive seminars trying to figure it out. I booked sessions with other psychics promising to deliver answers for my search. But none of them could.

I decided to try meditation. Specifically, recorded past life regressions and deep trance guided meditations. Some recordings I found from the Monroe Institute were the most effective. It was like boarding the rocket ship of consciousness expansion.

I learned to project my consciousness, a practice that felt vaguely familiar from my childhood. This allowed me to start meeting my guides in meditation. For a while, we met in the darkness. Just an empty void of nothingness other than telepathy. Imagine complete blackness where only sounds exist. I would ask them for help with issues I was experiencing, both in my personal life and with clients. Over time, I started to see them as plasmic balls of light. They were actually taking shape when we met in the darkness. They were the most vibrant luminescent shade of fuchsia I had ever seen. In fact, I have never seen anything like this color on Earth. It was absolutely stunning. I didn't want to look away. They would float in the void, in a circular shape, and communicate with me.

I had one meditation where I came to them with a deep emotional pain I was experiencing. We formed our circle in the darkness, and from each orb of light, two yellow spiraling light threads began to link between each of us. The light threads looked like DNA, and they began moving at an incredible speed around the circle. Each light orb that spiraling light passed through infused their strength and the intensity was something I've since tried but failed to put into words. It felt like an electric current coursing through each of us, gaining momentum and intensity with every pass through a guide—they were amplifying the power. And this current was love. The kind of love that drops you to your knees.

Eventually, the guides started to appear in the darkness with faces. Their faces were blurry, but had large eyes and their bodies faded out before reaching down to where one would typically expect feet. The more clear their faces became and the more bipedal shape they took, the more their fuschia color faded out. They began to appear more green-gray in this form.

A few months into my deep trans mediations, The Five started to cast holographic images in the middle of the circle for me to see and learn more. I had asked them what their names were and they answered with a collective sound, something I could not repeat if I tried. I told them I'd have to make "The Five" official as their name, and they agreed that this would be acceptable. A side note that may be of interest to some is that they have no sense of humor. Laughter is not a part of their makeup.

I could ask them about a problem a client was experiencing that I wanted spiritual support with, and The Five would suspend an image in their circle, holographic in nature, that would grant me insight on the appropriate solution. They still use this tactic to this day.

It's worth noting that The Five appeared for me in an order that I could handle. If they had first revealed themselves to me as figures with dark eyes hovering in a void sharing holographic images of current events in my life, I may have questioned my sanity. It would have been an overload for me. Instead, they first made contact as a soft whisper that was only vaguely distinguishable from my intuition. Like the voice I heard under the tree in Thailand. As I started to understand them more through my intense meditations, they slowly began to reveal more and more about themselves. I believe that for many of us, this gradual relationship development with our guides is by design. We need to mentally be able to handle what we're experiencing. This is also the reason I encourage others to start really examining their intuition and the subtle guidance they're experiencing. Chances are, there's a lot more where that came from.

Meeting with The Five in the astral realm takes work. I hear from them all the time, just like I do the spirit of any deceased I am connecting to. But if I want to see them, to circle up with them for deeper healing or guidance, I have to go through a rigorous meditative practice. During this practice, I am literally shifting my vibration and projecting my consciousness out of this realm.

It can take up to an hour to meet The Five through meditation. The first twenty-minutes are devoted to achieving a deeply relaxed state, then roughly ten minutes are devoted to shifting my consciousness to a vibration that matches theirs. The amount of time I spend with them is undetermined. When I am ready to "come back," I take a careful, slow process of return.

One time I fell asleep before I intentionally descended from the mediation and grounded back into my body. I was sleeping over at my boyfriend's house (my now husband, Neil) and woke him in the middle of the night to tell him that I was with his grandfather on the other side and that his grandfather had a lot to say. For the next two hours I told Neil everything his grandfather, Martin, was telling me. There were details down to the exact score of a tennis match that Martin watched Neil play and described to me as "the time of his life." It was one of the most deeply connected medium sessions I've ever led. But it was exhausting and I was teetering between realms for most of the next day too. This may sound like a wonderful state to exist in, transitioning without control between two worlds, but I can assure you, it isn't. I've since learned to always take the mindful process back to my body and my "humanness."

I often come out of more intense meditations either crying or with a nose bleed, the physical toll apparent. I've asked The Five why they can't appear for me as they do in meditations with less work required on my part and they said it's by intentional design. Going through the process is important as it allows the physical body to acclimate in phases, and slowly. Were I to connect with them instantly like this, it would "blow out a fuse" for my physical self. They explained that it's better this way. Otherwise, telepathy is the least physically disturbing manner of connection for my body.

The Five have confirmed in my meditative state that I was their form before incarnating on Earth. I asked them why we've stayed connected and their answer was cryptic, but that I am here to do "vibrational" work and that I am also not separate from them the way I believe I am as a human. "My belief system does not allow the entirety of the explanation," they have quoted to me.

My twin guides are different from The Five. I don't get the sense that I've been with them on other planets before, like I do The Five. I believe that they are more like soul teachers, here for me in this life to conquer specific things I'm working on as my human self, Jackie. I feel that I have been with them for many lives, but always with me as a physical being and them as ethereal beings.

I know that I met them in physical form once in Spain. I was studying abroad one summer during my undergrad. I went out to celebrate a local holiday, El Noche de San Juan, which involves a massive beach party with lots of drinking up until the hour of midnight. When the clock strikes twelve, everyone throws three things into the fire, then runs to jump over three waves in the ocean. You write down things that you want to get rid of on paper, and these are what you throw into the fire.

I was really unhappy during this study abroad program. I felt bullied by the other girls on the trip. This was not uncommon for me to experience, as I've shared that I often feel socially odd. Whether I was cognizant of it or not, there was no doubt that I was just wired differently than a lot of my peers. During this trip, this social separation was especially isolating as I didn't have any other friends or family around me in a foreign country.

I was pretty drunk by the time midnight rolled around.

I wanted to escape extreme discomfort and enjoy myself that night. I was excited by the ritual, and I followed the locals without much thought. I threw my three things into the fire, then ran out to the waves to make my three jumps. I leapt over the three waves, but then I just kept going. There were a few others ahead of me that were swimming out too, and I was feeling happy, carefree, and didn't want the feeling to end.

But before I knew it, I couldn't touch the bottom. A large wave came over me and I was swiftly pulled out to sea, my submerged body caught in a strong undercurrent. I came up for air and was fighting to stay afloat. It was only then that I realized how drunk I was. My coordination was off and I was quickly fatigued. Each wave that came over me seemed to only push me out further. It was pitch black around me and I couldn't get my bearings, nor see the shore anymore.

I felt tired, but in a way that's difficult to put into words. My body was tired, but even more so, my soul was tired. The more I tried to swim, the more exhaustion set in. After a while, I simply stopped fighting. It was a somber release of struggle, allowing myself to surrender into the ocean around me. I tilted my gaze up to the sky. The moon looked full. I watched the light of the moon fracture through the water as my face fully submerged and my body began to sink. I was motionless, staring at the fractal moon.

"This is what it feels like," I remember thinking, both interested and strangely relieved as I continued downwards underwater. What still strikes me about the incident was how relaxing the surrender was. I had a deep sense that I was finally going home.

Then a hand reached from above and grabbed me. I felt kicking and commotion. My head surfaced and I heard two boys speaking to each other. I laughed.

I still feel at odds with myself to this day that in that moment, I laughed.

One of them wrapped his arms around me and started kicking on his back. He and the other were shouting for quite some time. Eventually I started to hear music from the shore. Then I felt my feet graze sand. I stood up. I ran back towards the bonfire, still laughing.

When I reached the bonfire, I realized that I didn't recognize anyone. And all my things were missing. The two boys grabbed me by my arm and started dragging me down the beach. I must have been swept sideways in the ocean too because I was four or five bonfires away from my group. When we got there, I started trying to tell the other students what had just happened. It was loud and everyone was drunk. Nobody was paying attention to me.

The boys approached me again, frantically, and started helping collect my things. My shirt was missing but I had a linen skirt with a draw string that I could pull up as a dress. It had holes burned in it from embers of the cracking fire. They handed me my purse and flip flops and started leading me away from the bonfire, across the sand dunes, and back to the pathway to the street. From there, I could take the subway home. The twins were speaking to me the entire time, but I didn't recognize any words they were saying. I just assumed I was that drunk. A few others from the group were leaving at the same time. As we came through the sidewalk path onto the street, I turned to talk to the twins. But they weren't there.

"Where did those two guys go?" I asked my friend beside me.

"Which guys?"

"The ones that walked us over here?"

"I didn't see any guys."

"The two Spanish guys? That were with us from the bonfire? They walked over here with us."

"We were just following you," he replied, adamantly.

No one else saw them. Even when we all got to class the next Monday. I asked everyone I could, but no one saw the twins.

Either two complete strangers or two materialized guides saved my life that night. I've never felt the need to decide which it was.

But I have seen the same twins in my mediations since that night on the beach. I've named them Jacob and Michael, simply because those are the first names that came to me when I thought of them. They are playful energies, but organized and stern. I feel them when I am going through bouts of doubt, particularly around my career. They keep me on track, committed to my work with their guidance and support. Unlike The Five, Jacob and Michael use laughter. They often relay snarky, but teasing messages to me. While dedicated and serious, they are capable of playfulness.

Then there is Aranka. The ultimate guide. I sense that I have worked with her from the beginning of my energy creation. Through all lives and all forms of incarnation. She is shades of violet, indigo, fuchsia, and purple. Most of the time, she appears through my meditations as a plasmic light form. I've also seen her as a violet light-bird and once I asked to see her face. It was ornate, almost like a Mardi Gras mask, and her size was immeasurable. Most of my experience of Aranka has come through meditative connection, though after I understood who she was, I recognized different times in my life when she had been there but I was unaware. Like most things, when it comes to our guides, if we don't know what to look for, we probably won't see it at all.

Aranka is so sacred to me that I find her the most difficult to write about. But there's one story that I don't mind sharing. There was a short period of my life when I was numbing with substances the most, that I experienced a great deal of anxiety. My grandfather, whom I had adored, had just died and I was not in a good mental space. It was during graduate school and I had taken a trip home to Texas to spend time with my grandfather right before his passing. I had just been released from the emergency room, where I took myself out of suspicion that someone had dropped acid in my Diet Coke. Upon examination by the doctors, it turns out that I was having a severe panic attack. I know now that part of my anxiety was caused by trying to tune out my connection, and part of it was purely from the deep sadness I felt about the loss of my grandfather. I couldn't get my mind right.

Late that night, I wept in my bed. I was scared, uncomfortable, and afraid that the anxiety would return. I was crying out through internal prayer to any kind of God that might be listening. I was begging for mercy and emotional relief. I didn't know who or what I was talking to, but I was desperate for help.

"God," I prayed, "If you're real, please show yourself to me," I asked as I rolled onto my stomach and buried my face in my hands, weeping.

That is when I saw Aranka's face. A woman. And she was a force–both bold and delicate. The most stunning thing I'd ever seen. I was deeply confused by her image. At that point in my life, I'd never considered that "God" could be female. But I saw her.

I don't think Aranka is everyone's God. I think she is a unique guide, connected to me and possibly some others on Earth. But she is my main guide and is likely the closest manifestation to the ultimate source that I work with. Because in the end, I believe that all my guides originate from the same energy source.

The last note I'll share about my guides is that I'm often amused by who comes to greet me in my meditations. I know that if Aranka shows up, I'll be working on some major spiritual work. If I find Jacob and Michael, I know that what I'm working on may be more earthly, egotistical, or even career related. The Five almost exclusively support my mediumship connection work.

TELLING MY FAMILY

I hesitated to open up about my psychic mediumship connection abilities with my family the most. And hesitation is an understatement. I was absolutely petrified.

Mustering the courage to come out fully and openly to my closest family wasn't a decision made from a place of confidence, but rather out of utter fear. After relying solely on word-of-mouth referrals and a one-page website for many years, I decided to expand my reach by building out my website and engaging in a PR campaign orchestrated by a friend in the industry. I aimed to make my services accessible to those who had suffered a profound loss. Soon enough, I found myself being sought out by a diverse assortment of people—celebrities, executives, television producers, and more. I began appearing on podcasts, in documentaries, and even in books.

I was haunted by the paranoia that my family might stumble upon some media coverage about me and discover the truth without my disclosure. If I could have hidden it from them with certainty, I might never have revealed what I was doing. This fear is all too real for many who engage in any form of public exposure, especially in the realm of spirituality and energy healing practices. We're consumed by dread over what others will think.

For me, sharing with my family was the scariest step of them all. I'm not even particularly close to my family, which adds another layer of complexity to the fear I felt. But I couldn't fathom a situation that would, at the time, make me feel more alone and sad on this planet than to be banished by my family. Despite our lack of closeness, I found a false sense of comfort in the absence of outright rejection from them.

I was raised in a household steeped in strong Christian beliefs, with Presbyterian roots on my mother's side and Baptist traditions on my father's. In this environment, communicating with the deceased was viewed with suspicion, as a form of witchcraft, or potentially evil. The teachings I encountered warned against risking connections with dark forces or inadvertently summoning demons. It was implied that such connections should be left to pastors and other church leaders who possessed special knowledge and authority. While prayer was deemed acceptable for me, anything beyond prayer required supervision and guidance from religious authorities. Which was rather funny to me, since my abilities were accepted by my father's side of the family, as long as they were framed in a context aligned with the Holy Spirit and not labeled as psychic.

Despite my deep love for my family and appreciation for

the moral principles upheld by many religions, I reached a point where I could no longer deny the truth of my experiences as a medium. One evening, while dining with an aunt at a burger restaurant, I made a spontaneous decision to share my mediumship experiences with her. It wasn't a planned confession—in fact, it went against my better judgment at the time. However, as our conversation turned to my upcoming trip to a conference in San Diego to study with a renowned Medical Medium, my aunt asked me about the purpose of my travels. In that moment, I felt an internal urge to speak my truth. And so, despite my reservations, I did.

While talking with my aunt, I experienced an odd physical reaction. I felt as if there was a one-ton oscillator in my stomach. It was a visceral spasm— an uncontrollable and relentless shaking from my solar plexus. It started the moment I felt the urge to tell the truth, and even after confessing my mediumship to my aunt, I continued to shake for at least an hour afterward.

I don't recall her reaction at all. In fact, I think I sugar-coated the truth, telling her that I believed I had "intuitive" abilities and that I was going to explore this possibility further. I didn't mention that I had been practicing as a psychic medium with undeniable accuracy and a quickly growing clientele.

As diluted as that initial confession was, I recognize it as a turning point because I released something in that moment. I let go of something that wasn't mine —the heightened stigma surrounding mediumship—and embraced the truth of my identity. I am a psychic medium. And I believe that internal oscillation I felt was a somatic release of trauma, fear, and embarrassment that often accompanies embracing one's true self.

But if I hadn't started with that one relative, I wouldn't have learned that not only was I okay, no matter how she responded, but that I could also more fully own who I really am. This confession started a pattern throughout my life of me simply letting myself just be who I am, regardless of how others felt about it. And I don't think I would be where I am now if I hadn't found the courage to behave differently that night at the burger restaurant. This experience was the beginning of a path I continue to walk to this day; one where telling the truth about what is going on inside of me and the abilities that I have is my norm, regardless of the receiver of my message.

I continued to offer my family a diluted version of the truth at first, claiming I was practicing Reiki energy work and intuitive connection sessions. Which is humorous considering I just stated that I'd made a decision to be myself, regardless of how anyone felt about it. But I simply didn't want to get into it with my family. Thankfully, no one probed further into the details, since I was making it all up.

It turned out, my fear was not unfounded. A lot of my family did not approve. Though no one confronted me directly, they spoke disparagingly of me in front of other family members, who then relayed their words back to me. I was condemned for what they perceived as dabbling in the devil's work, deemed wrong and evil according to their interpretation of the Bible. They warned of impending trouble with demons. Some of them chose to sever ties with me completely, and I've never managed to mend those relationships.

It was an incredibly isolating time for me. Despite knowing the beauty of the service I was providing and the profound impact I was having on my clients' lives, I felt a deep sense of loneliness. Over time, I learned to focus on the beauty of my life and my work with spirit. I came to realize that while the security offered by our biological families is comforting, it is not essential for experiencing profound peace and connection in life.

In addition, serving as the conduit for such profound messages from spirit expanded my capacity to experience deep love. There's a unique closure that comes from being able to convey "last words" when someone passes unexpectedly. This is the essence of what mediumship sessions offer people. They give comfort and help individuals recognize that life continues after death, albeit in a different form. Alongside closure, there's the transmission of unconditional love in sessions. I became a vessel for both the ferocity and beauty of the most profound messages of love. They not only healed those who received them but also eased much of the pain or loneliness I felt.

For many of us, embracing our spiritual truth can lead to a divide between ourselves and our biological families. I don't feel it's my place to give advice to those facing this decision; whether to conceal their deepest truths or not. I can only share the choice I made. Initially, I was devastated. I longed to prove myself to my family, amongst other doubters, and show them that my work was rooted in pure, loving intentions. I was desperate to feel a sense of belonging within my earthly family.

I learned that who I am as a spiritual being has nothing to do with anyone except me and Spirit. I can't manage anyone's perception of me, regardless of how hard I try or how truly loving my intentions are. Self-worth implies that it comes from self. Not from others. And when I was able to fully and truly integrate this universal law, I was able to let go of the need to win over my biological family's approval.

The release of our need for external validation is important for our spiritual growth. It requires self-acceptance, which opens a space for the expansion of our abilities. I believe that our capacity to perceive anything, ethereal or physical, is limited by the receptors we have available and ready for use. And when our bodies are burdened with blocks, fears, and doubts, they occupy all our receptors for spiritual connection. As we clear these obstacles, we open ourselves to the unseen. We free up innate receptors for Spirit. I became a better medium when I fully and completely released the fear of what other people would think of me.

This would also explain a few things: like why moving stagnant energies through yoga was such a key part of my journey, why my initial confession to my family triggered a somatic response, and why facing fear was vital for my psychic development. I was releasing negative emotions that were clogging my receptors.

Reflecting on your life, you've likely encountered pivotal moments—unplanned instances where you became acutely aware of your higher self and thereby chose a different path. You confronted fear, sat with it, and it didn't overwhelm you. These moments of inner awareness and choice shape our lives in profound ways.

Regarding my position of my past religious upbringing, my current beliefs are flexible and unrestricted by the necessity to declare any specific affiliations. They evolve continuously as I interact with more spirits and acquire new knowledge. I am guided by my connection to a loving, unseen force that transcends any single doctrine or specific path. I've relinquished the need to grasp the absolute "truth" in this lifetime and instead, consistently embrace the experiential truth of my journey. Because the one truth I know for certain, is that nobody will know exactly what's happening on the other side until we die. And by then, it won't matter.

MY MENTORS & SOBRIETY

People looking for help with their abilities or spiritual struggles are commonly very interested in the mentors, teachers, and healers that I worked with. I completely understand the interest. Unfortunately, I can't share specific details about my teachers. At least not through a book. Not because of some rule, but because of how it all works.

Our teachers are divinely guided by a force both greater than myself and far beyond my comprehension. My teachers sort of just "appeared" along my path at the precise right moment. I would think to myself, "I really need someone to teach me about this experience that I'm having," and then the next day a friend would mention a teacher they found that had really helped them with that exact need I had. That friend would then share the teacher's contact information with me and I would reach out to connect. Or I'd come across a podcast interviewing a specialist in that exact topic later that afternoon. Maybe I'd walk into a bookstore and see precisely the book I needed to help me learn more on display at the front stand. This perfectly-timed divine guidance shows up in many ways.

I once met a friend, Tim, in New York City for nachos at a casual Mexican food restaurant on the Upper West Side of the city. We were sitting at a table outside on Columbus Avenue. I was terrified to share about what was happening with me, for fear that my friend would judge or ridicule me. I was at a point in my psychic development where I was frequently seeing myself as an alien type being in my meditations. The visions were clear and the setting and environment were consistent. Each time that I would connect to this version of myself through meditation, I would remember more and more. I use the word "remember" with intention, as I did not feel like I was discovering something, but instead, that I was connecting to a past experience.

Throughout our meal, I kept feeling an internal nudge to talk to Tim about it. There came a point in our casual conversation where I could organically introduce the topic and, despite my fear, I shared about my meditations with him. He asked me a few questions about the landscape I saw, what I looked like, and if I could recall any other details.

He looked genuinely amused by it all. "Wait a second," he asked me, then turned to pull his phone from his bag hanging on his chair. He scrolled through his phone for quite some time, a broad smile across his face.

"Here, right here," he pointed to text on the phone. "Read this entire page."

It was a digital version of Yogananda's book, *The Autobiography of a Yogi*, and every single thing that I had described, to the final detail, was depicted inside this book.

"There's no way," I shook my head in disbelief. "What a weird coincidence," I stated.

"It's not a coincidence," he sounded appalled. "The yogis have known what we're all discovering. They know about shapeshifting, bi-location, reincarnation, and the rematerializing of the great dead masters. All the planets and various forms of life. The yogis have known. You should read the book," he finished.

I went home and ordered the book immediately. And once it arrived, it changed my life, page by page. It was the exact teaching that I needed for that exact leg of my journey.

And this is not something I can predict or recommend to others. At least not through the words of a book. Perhaps this book is resting in your palms at the perfect timing for the highest and best spiritual growth for you at this exact moment on your spiritual path.

My best advice for spiritual seekers is no matter how hard things get or how much you're suffering, keep going. Talk about your experiences. Ask friends for help. Set your intentions to find your own highest and best teachers. Do not give up and do not hold back. Ask the universe for help. Because we get what we ask for. That is the most spiritual instruction I can offer through a book. When the student is ready, the teacher appears.

I wholeheartedly believe that choosing sobriety has impacted my psychic clarity. Having the willingness to sort out my emotional turmoil, the openness to follow the whispers of guidance into deep meditative states, and the courage to face my fears despite the emotional ramifications have without a doubt all contributed to my connection.

I encourage those seeking as I was and as I still am to work hard to understand themselves. Even if you feel like an outsider socially, don't turn on yourself. It's far better to be a loner who knows the truth of who and what they are than to be someone who fits in but has abandoned their deepest truths.

OTHER FEARS

I'm still working on certain necessary healings from my psychic abilities and professional mediumship. Consider the aftermath of conducting nearly 2,000 medium sessions with clients desiring to reconnect with their departed loved ones. It's an immersion in death. You start to see death everywhere. I can tell you six ways from Sunday how one might experience an untimely death in any common situation. While it's not funny at all, I've learned to bring some levity to my experiences so I don't break down mentally and physically.

My husband is fifteen minutes later than I expected from a trip to the grocery store and I find myself pacing the kitchen at home, consumed by thoughts of my client's husband who suffered a stroke on his way home from work. Or the tragic fate of another client's cousin who slipped and hit his head after retrieving his forgotten jacket from a restaurant.

Even on what could be the most perfect day, after enjoying a delightful breakfast together before he sets off for the store, I can't shake the ominous thoughts. I imagine him admiring our beautiful surroundings as he loads the car, driving off distracted by the gorgeous day, only to veer slightly off the drive, just like the motorcyclist whose life ended so abruptly. I'll start texting my husband repeatedly as I become increasingly frantic with each minute that he does not respond.

Finally, I receive a text back from him. "I'm still shopping. What is your issue?" At least that's how he would initially respond to my anxiety, early on in our relationship.

"I was worried something happened to you," I explained when he returned home.

I had to really let him inside my head and the way I processed things. This is what I mean when I say it's hard to be vulnerable and raw. It was challenging for me to allow someone I loved inside my thought process, to confess all the ways that my work–the work I chose and still choose daily–messes me up inside sometimes.

He probably never thought about what it's like to constantly be aware of the many ways one could die. It's not just about the physical aspects but also the emotional toll and the impact it has on the lives of those left behind. I often found myself planning for the worst, thinking about how I would cope if something happened to him. As I paced around our kitchen, I couldn't shake the fear of a police officer arriving at our door with news of his death. I can't fully describe the feeling, but it became even more intense when we had our son.

My husband has become much more patient with me over time. Additionally, I've gained a new perspective that has helped me alleviate much of my fear. Through numerous meditations and conversations with my guides, I've come to understand that death is inevitable for all of us. Something that should be apparent yet has taken me some work to accept. Instead of dwelling on the fear of death, what truly matters is our commitment to living fully. It's about embracing deep love, finding joy in everyday experiences, and remaining grateful for every moment we have.

And because of the reality that death can come for any one of us at any time, my husband and I have a plan if one of us goes unexpectedly. I told him the signs I will send him from the spirit world when I am making contact and he has shared his signs with me. People wonder if the signs they see and feel from past loved ones, like songs that play spontaneously, butterflies that appear, or symbols that show up, are in fact from the other side. They usually are. And with my husband, I don't want there to be any question that the other is connecting.

This next fear is not related to my experience as a medium, but instead to my personal experience with a tragic loss. And I want to share about it because I've learned from my sessions that people often develop seemingly unrelated fears after a loved one dies tragically.

I lost my brother-in-law to a senseless act of violence which I shared in an earlier chapter about my distraught Thanksgiving day. The events surrounding his death shocked me. It was sudden and gruesome. After his passing, I found myself unable to take my foot off of the break of my car after shifting the gear into the parked position. I would put the car in park, then sit there, the brake still depressed, in a mild sense of panic for moments or possibly even minutes. I would then slightly release the brake and slam it back down, not trusting that the car would stay put, despite checking multiple times that it was in fact still in park. I would summon a great deal of courage then just close my eyes and release the brake, waiting in anticipation to see if the whole thing actually worked. Did the park position of my gear-shifter actually mean that I was in park? Could I even trust it?

This brother-in-law passed away eight years ago and I still have anxiety when I put my car in park. I couldn't pretend to explain this. But I can share that these kinds of fears are common after a tragic loss and manifest without any kind of predictable pattern. I've had a client who could no longer put quarters in a laundry machine after losing her mother without a crippling sense of panic. One client couldn't open the windows of his house, even though he loved a fresh breeze after his brother died in a skiing accident. The fears are without explanation and don't have logical ties to the cause of death or potential threat presented by the fear. My brother-in-law was stabbed to death. That doesn't logically correlate to my car lurching forward while in park, but I am still to this day afraid to release my foot. I don't understand the fears, but again, I can report that they are common.

There is one more fear that people are often curious about. And that's the fear of running into something evil or dark in my connection time. This is not something I give much thought to anymore. Because of course, there is darkness, and of course I see terrible things "out there" when I am connected. But I don't engage with them. Or if I do, I've come to understand they are often aspects of myself simply asking for a hug. My fears are things that I am afraid of, possibilities created by my mind, that need my attention.

There was one event that helped me integrate this truth. Because in the early stages of my mediumship practice and deep transcendental meditations, I often ran into dark, scary things. They disturbed me and if I had allowed it, they would have deterred me from deeper practice. One of my teachers, Jerry Wills, instructed me to first ask them to leave. And if that didn't work, to eat them by visualizing a sharp, quick inhalation where I would suck them into my energy field.

Every book that I read and the human guides that I had worked with so far were teaching me that one of the biggest suppressants of human potential is the programming that tells us that we are not powerful. And we receive this subtle programming our entire lives: We must bow to pray. We need a "leader" to help us with our relationship to the heavens. Schools are better than our parents for instruction. Our imagination is silly. You have to work hard at the American dream to own various things.

I became aware of all the ways we are told that we are not capable. I wanted the kind of power that Jerry was teaching about. I wanted to believe in myself and fear nothing.

I set my mind to challenge these entities next time I encountered one. They often visited me in the moments before falling into deep sleep or coming out of sleep into a fully awake state. One night, as I was shifting from awake to asleep, a dark visitor came. He was actually green, not dark, but I felt terrified of his negative energy. I was lying in my bed in the moments before sleep and this green being appeared outside my window. I was on the seventh floor of a building, so the fact that he was at my window was scary enough. He had long, skinny, Grinch-like fingers with something solid as marble at each finger-tip. He used this hard surface of his finger to tap on the glass of my window. The sound was unnatural to come from a hand. It was terrifying.

I remembered what Jerry said. I asked him forcefully to leave. But he did not. He stayed at the window, hovering and tapping. I was frozen in my bed, unable to move my body out of my pre-sleep state. I tried to visualize myself sucking him into my energy, but he was solid matter. In my mind, I had planned to suck in an immaterial entity. I couldn't make the exercise work as planned because I didn't *believe* I could inhale solid matter. He kept taunting me, tapping slowly with his long, creepy fingers.

And then I got angry. I was pissed, actually. It reminded me of all the times I'd been ostracized for being different. I summoned a strength from deep inside myself and suddenly, my astral body sat up. I threw my feet over the edge of the bed and stomped my way over to the window. I threw the window open and grabbed this being by the shoulders. My strength had no bounds–he was no match for me.

I drug him inside my window and hurled him onto the massage table that I kept set up for clients who came to me for energy work. He was sitting, with his legs over the side of the table, and we were face-to-face. I looked him square in the eye, shook him by the shoulders, and demanded, "What. Do. You. Want?"

He looked at me, green eyes glowing. No answer.

I shook him again with a strength that astounded me, "Answer me right now."

His chin quivered. He softened. "A hug," he cowered.

He wanted a hug? I was taken aback. This green monster had been taunting me for years. He made me afraid to go to sleep at times. His hovering shook me to my core. And all he wanted was to be embraced?

I looked him in the eyes again and the oddest thing happened. I saw myself. I saw a pain and fear that was unmistakably the exact same as mine. I drew him into my chest, rested my hand on the back of his head, and I held him.

Then he vanished. Simply dissipated. I never saw him again. And my fear of the darkness has not been the same ever since. Truth be told, I have not had any run-ins with beings since that night.

I believe our fears are not actually entities or energy beings, but instead are outcast elements of ourselves. We create them and without our making they do not exist. If we want to "unmake" them, we must square off with them, look them in the face, and call them back home— into our being just as Jerry instructed.

To close: I always assure those who are concerned with bumping into "bad things" that despite the darkness I've encountered in the unseen world, nothing has come close to the kind of evil present here on Earth.

AN ODD EVENT

A few of my childhood experiences with visitors started to come full circle on Thanksgiving just a few years before writing this book. I traveled to my sister's house to spend the holiday with my family. It was a nice, uneventful few days together with good food and lots of warm fires going in the early winter of Colorado, where my sister was living.

I had been at my sister's house for a few days and was packing my bag to head back home. I felt my sister being a little awkward, lurking around the room as I was packing, pretending to busy herself. She pulled something from a drawer and moved closer to me. Then she handed me a book.

"Will you do me a favor and please just read this with an open mind?" she asked, reluctantly.

I stared at her. I could feel that there was more behind the request. I thought she had some kind of confession to make and wanted to prime me with this book.

"I'll read it but why are you being so weird?"

"Just finish the book and then tell me what you remember about our childhood."

I'm not the type for these kinds of situations because I want to talk about things right now. Not anticipate something for weeks or months, as the scenarios I'll create in my head are ten-fold worse and weirder than what the reality typically pans out to be.

"Why don't we talk about it now?" I pressed.

"Well," she hesitated. Jessica was being awkward. I wanted to leave right then and there. "Do you remember the night the burglars came?"

I knew exactly what she was talking about, nothing more needed to be said.

"Yes."

"Do you remember anything weird about that night?"

"I do."

"Have you ever thought maybe it wasn't burglars?"

"No," I lied. "Maybe a little. Some of it doesn't make sense, but I just figured I was so young. I probably don't remember it right"

The truth was, I'd thought about it more times than I cared to admit. I remember waking up on the floor between my bed and the wall. My mother was frantically calling out my name, looking for me up and down the hallway. I felt mad at her, so I didn't respond. I just listened to her desperation. I must have been three-years-old.

Before waking up on the floor, I remember bright lights outside the windows. It was as if someone had planted stadium lights at each of our windows and flicked them all on simultaneously. There was a powerful wind too, and the front door was swinging open and closed. There was so much happening, unnatural amounts of commotion, but I was paralyzed. I could see it all, but I couldn't move. Then I saw a flash of darkness. When I opened my eyes again, I was on the floor by my bed, listening to my mother, with a feeling of anger towards her.

Our dog was barking and my sister was upset. My mom finally turned on my bedroom light and saw me on the floor. She picked me up and carried me into the living room, where my sister was wrapped in a blanket, crying.

"Someone tried to break in," my mom explained, still visibly distraught. "I must have left the door unlocked."

My sister said she was hiding under the blanket in the recliner in the living room, and tried to freeze so they wouldn't notice her. I remember the exact blanket. I believe it was made by my great grandmother and was crocheted from hollow octagon shapes. It was by no means opaque. I recall assessing how not-hidden-at-all my sister would have been. My sister said she only saw fast movement. But eventually my dog started barking and ran to the door to attack, waking us all up.

I frequently reconsider the intricate details of the events that unfolded that night. How I felt upset with my mom, how odd the bright lights would have been for someone trying to break in. Whoever it was, they were sure making a lot of commotion for someone trying to be stealth. Then there was the fact that the lights didn't wake my mom up. Or that my dog didn't immediately bark. Why was I on my bed one moment and the floor the next? Did my sister actually believe she was hidden?

My mom had a motion detecting alarm system put in our house shortly after this incident. And a lifelong fear of being kidnapped in the night set in for me. Something I wouldn't understand for many years to come.

I refocused my thoughts back to the present moment. I grabbed the book from my sister.

The Forgotten Promise by Sherry Wilde.

"Please just give it a chance," Jessica asked again.

"I said I would," I responded, feeling annoyed. She's always dramatic.

"You were always better at projecting from this dimension," my sister added. "You tried to teach me but I couldn't."

I vividly recall internally nodding with fervor, though outwardly displaying no visible reaction to my sister. At that moment, I couldn't help but think, "Welp, here we go, diving headfirst into the family discussion. Straight into the deep end." I decided to put an end to any further conversation.

"What are you talking about? What is going on? Are you serious? Are you drunk?" I demanded.

"No. Just read the book. And try to remember your own childhood."

I was experiencing a whirlwind of unanswered questions, each one clamoring for attention yet suppressed beneath a veneer of stoicism. It's a peculiar paradox; the simultaneous desire to both discuss and avoid a conversation we've longed for and needed. Amidst this internal turmoil, my mind was flooded with countless confessions burning to break free–tales of my experiences, memories, and discoveries. Despite the undeniable amount of evidence of a reality beyond conventional understanding, I found myself silenced by my fear, reluctant to unravel the intricate web of falsehoods that were holding reality as I knew it together. It was a battle being waged within the depths of my psyche.

Because while I was in the middle of my psychic reawakening at the time, I was still feeling deeply uncomfortable discussing my abilities with my family. This reluctance is a common struggle for many psychically gifted individuals, again because we fear being ostracized or labeled as mentally unstable. Consequently, we often conceal these abilities from those closest to us, dreading the potential for judgment, ridicule, or even downright rejection.

Plus, my sister has a tendency to escalate situations at the slightest provocation. Aware of her habit of intensifying discussions, I let the conversation end there and packed the book away in my suitcase.

The book, *The Forgotten Promise*, is about the author's lifelong interactions with beings from another world. I recommend it for anyone who suspects that they too may have been visited or contacted by off-planet species. I read it in the two days following my Thanksgiving trip and recall feeling a sense of relief. Parts of Wilde's story are familiar to me. A lot of her experiences are nothing like my own. More than anything, her willingness to share the truth paved a path for myself and I'm sure countless others to share their experiences with less trepidation.

When I called my sister to discuss the book, we realized that we both remembered parts of our childhood in the same way, which was different from how the adults in our families remembered them. We both remember the night of the "break in" the same way. There was so much commotion. Then a flash of darkness, then my mother waking in a panic. A few years later, I would decide to undergo hypnosis to try to recall more about this night. I will share about this in a further chapter.

NEIL

Shortly after moving home to Dallas from New York City, I met my husband–in the wild–at a rooftop bar. We live in a time where a lot of couples meet through dating apps, so I think it's a prime example of just another possible small intervention from the other side that we met by chance and organically. Despite all of the spiritual work I had done to straighten out my inner self, I still had defects. I believe my late grandfather played a role in guiding our union, appearing at pivotal moments along the way, and ultimately influencing our decision to marry. He was certainly present during my decision-making process to follow the prophetic dream I'd had just prior to moving home. He kept whispering, "Pack your bags, Baby Girl," a nickname he called me my whole life.

One evening about a year into dating, Neil and I got into a severe argument. I was somewhat protective by nature and tended to shut down or even leave if my intimate relationships led to an argument or an intense disagreement. I have many ridiculously funny stories of just leaving when I was too uncomfortable. And I wouldn't do it like a normal dysfunctional person. I'd lay in bed and wait until my partner fell asleep. Then I'd tip-toe around, gather my things, and slip out in the night.

I don't even remember what my husband and I were arguing about that night, but I asked him to leave me alone and go to bed. I told him that I had more important work to do and that I didn't care to continue with the argument. In all transparency, I was emotionally underdeveloped in relationships and couldn't handle the feelings I was having and the threat I felt like I was under.

We were at his house, where he had graciously designated an entire room as my office. I had every intention of packing my bag and going to my house as soon as he was out of my sight, or even better—as soon as he was sleeping. I just wanted to get away from the intensity of my feelings and my fears.

I distinctly remember like it was yesterday looking down at my hands while sitting at my desk, taking a deep breath, and becoming exceptionally aware of the truth of my situation and the fact that I was running from something I needed to be stepping into and working through. I could feel my spirit nudging for my attention. It sounds like that little voice inside saying, "Hey, you sure you want to do this again?" And I think we all get nudges when we have an opportunity for growth if we make new choices.

When I become focused in the now, or bring my full awareness into the present moment, my mediumship connections become easy and frequent. I distinctly remember feeling my late grandfather's presence that night. He told me to get up and go be with Neil. "You get up right now," were his exact words.

But my fear kept telling me that this was too dangerous. Clearly sneaking out was the better decision. And it wasn't that I didn't want to work through things with Neil or with partners in my past, it was that my ego and fear always won—and I always left. Somehow, that night, my spirit overpowered every negative emotion, fear, and toxic pattern that I felt surging through my body.

And I found myself walking up the stairs to his bedroom, sitting down at the edge of the bed beside him, and asking to hold his hand. He looked shocked.

It was equally as wild for me, as I fundamentally believed that the argument was his fault and that he was wrong. And yet there I was, sitting with him, connecting with him, and wanting to work through it together. This was uncharted territory for me. And as small as this story may seem, I know that my life pivoted from that point forward. I made a decision from a different place within myself. One that I'd never known before or had never been able to find when I had looked for it in the past.

Rather than following a familiar path that led to dysfunctional relationships, my spirit guided me in a new direction, setting the stage for a significant shift in my life. This change ultimately paved the way for my marriage and the beginning of our beautiful little family.

I attribute some of this decision to feeling and sensing my late grandfather's guidance. He was right. And I believe that between his help and my own growing spiritual awareness, a new part of me woke up that night. I think Spirit is always guiding us to grow in loving, connected, beautiful ways. To hear from my relatives is uncommon for me. It is for a lot of mediums. We can connect for others but have a hard time for ourselves. So my grandfather's presence at these key moments of my life remains inexpressibly meaningful.

There was a specific detail that came through during my dream vision about the upcoming militant-like state of New York City that's another sweet part of Neil's and my union. I had very clearly received a message that the "world would drastically change on March 29th." It was a date that I had blocked in my calendar and even told some of my clients and closest friend's to be aware of.

Neil and I had been cultivating a friendship for several weeks leading up to the 29th of March. I had confided in him about how concerned I felt about this date. We were one-week into lockdowns, one-month into a stock market crash, and there was talk of impending doom coming from some of the underground channels that I follow for unbiased news. Not to mention the visions I'd seen of New York City, which hadn't started making total sense yet. We were very much in a waiting game as a nation, sitting out something nobody knew much about at the time.

I was scared about this "drastic world change" and could only imagine the worst case scenarios, despite my efforts to keep my energy positive. Neil suggested that I come to his place that afternoon and that we could cook a meal together and watch a Ram Dass documentary while we waited until midnight.

I agreed to join him. We made chicken wings and put

on the documentary. During the show, Neil asked if he could hold my hand. He said we could be together when the clock struck midnight. I did, and we made it. Nothing happened. It was uneventful and though I felt confused about how wrong I had been, I was relieved that we were okay and didn't have a new catastrophe to cope with.

When the movie ended, Neil told me that he wanted to, "be my boyfriend," a request that was so sweet and pure for both of us being in our late thirties. I agreed, and we have been together ever since.

My world did drastically change that day. Spirit was right. But it was for the better, and in the most beautiful way.

MEETING MOSS IN THE TUNNEL

Well, I gave birth to Moss and I was nowhere near finished with this book. My husband and I chose to have an unmedicated, natural, mostly unassisted delivery. When people ask me what my experience of giving birth was like, I often joke and tell them that I felt like I had been lied to. It was way worse than I could have planned or ever imagined. I thought that I was tough and believed I had a high tolerance for pain. But unmedicated childbirth proved me wrong. From my perspective, there are simply no words to relay to another human being the amount of pain a woman endures through labor and delivery. Perhaps this is why all the women that I had asked about their birthing experiences before having Moss had simply said, "It's pretty bad, but it's worth it." Many times during my twenty-four hours of labor, I both laughed and cried about my conclusion that I had been lied to.

Natural birth for me was soul shattering. I realized that I do not have a high tolerance for pain. With fear of sounding extreme, I'm not making light of the experience or joking in the slightest when I admit that I begged for death. There was a point, about forty-minutes before

Moss was delivered, that I desperately tried to reach The Five. I was pleading for help. I was convinced that my physical body simply could not withstand another contraction.

I started to demand that the two midwives take me to the hospital because I was going to get drugs. No one, I told them, should ever feel anything like this. It felt unsafe. Wrong.

Trying to keep me distracted, one of the midwives asked me from a scale of one to seven, where I was with my pain. "Seven?" I snarled. "I passed eleven three hours ago!"

She calmly took my aggression with a slight smile pursed behind her lips. It pissed me off at the time, but I now know that the midwives knew this meant Moss was coming very soon.

At one point, the midwives left me on my own in a warm bath. And while my body wasn't showing signs of being ready for birth, I could feel it in my deepest knowing, that Moss was coming soon. The pain became so intense, so consistent, that I inadvertently began to project my consciousness outside of my body. I saw no other way to deal with the pain than to force my spirit out of my body, though I was no longer capable of rational or intentional thought. It was the closest walk with Spirit I've ever taken. I was teetering between realms.

At one point, after projecting from my body, I started astrally searching the birthing center looking for the midwives. I felt that I was not in a physically safe condition to have been left on my own. I found them in the kitchen complaining about an appliance that had been replaced and discussing how they liked the old one more. One of the midwives was talking about her daughter and I saw that her daughter liked to take baths and soak in scented oils and salts. The other midwife was unmarried, but I caught visions of her in the future, married and with a young girl or at least a young child with braids. They were traveling with luggage. The midwife and her child were at the airport and they were taking a trip that they were excited about.

Then I launched from planet Earth. I entered a tunnel with quickly moving lights and colors, or I was quickly moving and the colors were passing by. There was no measure of time – I can't tell you if I was traveling for minutes, seconds, who knows. But suddenly I came to an abrupt stop and in front of me was an elderly, Asian male. He was withered and small but he was powerful. I could tell that he had mastered an energy practice in the realm of martial arts – he could maneuver energy and was a force to be feared. But he was so small and meager looking. He was headed for the direction from which I'd traveled – he was headed for Earth at the same speed in which I was headed out. He was traveling back to my body. This energy master and great sage was Moss.

He was determined, unstoppable. This soul was on a mission. He paid no mind to my presence. And then in a flash, I found myself back in my body.

"I need to push," I began coaching myself. I started screaming. The midwives entered the room and told me I wasn't quite ready for pushing but I said that I didn't care, I needed to push. It was time.

One of them sat down on the floor beside the birthing tub and told my husband that if he wanted to assist in catching the baby, he should take off his long sleeve shirt as his hands would be in the water. She told me that we were entering the fun part. And that if I felt it was time, then we would work on pushing together.

I pushed once.

"Okay, his head is out," said the midwife, calmly but clearly surprised.

"I need to be patient, now don't I?" I asked her.

"I don't know," she calmly responded, looking me softly in the eyes. I had asked for the least amount of intervention or assistance possible in my birthing plan and she was giving me what I had asked for.

I pushed again and felt a weird slosh, then the midwife handed me Moss. As I sat back against the side of the circular tub, my husband came from around the corner in a short sleeve shirt. His face went white and his jaw dropped.

"Is something wrong?" I asked, full of adrenaline and terrified by the look on his face.

I was feeling panicked because I knew things could go wrong with birth. I began to shuffle through negative possibilities I was aware of with birth–hemorrhaging, tearing, umbilical cord placement. I was spiraling out.

"He's here," he said. "You just had the baby," Neil stated, shocked. He was not there for my two-push birth. He was taking off his sweater while I had our son. We still laugh about this.

And that was about it. That's how Moss came. In the night, in the water.

When we went for our six-week check up with the midwives, I finally told them about my astral voyage and finding them in the kitchen. I share how I met Moss in what I've come to call the birth tunnel. And that our meeting had given me a cosmically infused strength to return to my physical body and bring him home—to Earth.

Both midwives laughed and confirmed that they probably were talking about the toaster, as they hated the new one and both believed that the old one was better. One midwife confirmed that she had a daughter who loved taking baths and added that she had just been to the store to buy her more oils and salts for soaking in the tub. I told the other midwife that I had seen visions of her in the future, traveling with her child. She was a little more surprised by this detail but said it would be a good thing. She was going the following weekend to meet her boyfriend's parents and wished that something more would come of their relationship, something like marriage.

Time will tell if Moss carries into this life what I saw of the soul's form. I can say one thing for sure, that boy loves sushi. The first time he had sushi, he was about ten-months-old and he ate it like he hadn't seen food in weeks. It was aggressive. As if he missed it. Moss also has a small blue birthmark on his back. Our medical provider told us that these are called Mongolian spots, and they typically only appear on children of Asian descent. Less than ten percent of caucasian babies present Mongolian spots.

I experienced an incredible, non-verbal union with Moss from the second I held him in my arms. When he was in my womb, I didn't really consider our separateness. Talking to myself was talking to him, because I felt that we were one.

But after delivery, the separation between us was physically complete. There was an energetic exchange between us that was intense, albeit completely effortless, as if he were still merged with my body. In the weeks following his birth, I found myself building up a resistance to our connection with each other. It became difficult for me to accept and trust how easily I could communicate with my little baby without words. I found myself struggling to concede something so powerful that I just didn't have to work for. Unlike the years of personal and spiritual work leading up to my mediumship connection, this union simply *was*.

Even though I was over a decade into my medium career and well established as a psychic at the time of his birth, I still needed to put effort into my psychic connection time with my clients. There is a process to my medium work and while I wouldn't say it was or is particularly difficult, it still requires focus and effort. But my connection with Moss was incessant and fluent.

This threw me for a loop. I found myself feeling undeserving of something so cogent that was this easy. I questioned my accuracy. I booked multiple sessions with one of my teachers, a Psych-K healer, in the first few weeks of his life to receive help on simply allowing the channel of connection between the two of us. I can't put my finger on exactly why I felt this way, but I share this experience in case other mothers find themselves in a similar position. All of the Psych-K healing work was focused on simply allowing the magnitude of our entanglement. Something about the ease of it all broke me into tiny pieces emotionally. It was as if I were staring Source in the face and wanted to close my eyes because the majesty of the experience was too much to receive.

Direct connection to the unseen can feel like that sometimes. Simultaneously humbling and shattering, we find ourselves in tears attempting to process everything we're perceiving. And yet, there's a sense of yearning at the same time. It's as if we've reconnected to something we've forgotten–something our souls know that we had to leave behind when we came to Earth to be human. This is what my connection to Moss made me feel and it's why I say becoming a mother is one of the most spiritually enhancing experiences I've ever had. I have learned to trust my connection in an entirely new way. It has reminded my soul about truths I needed to remember. Which has indirectly made me a better medium. Because I did learn to trust my connection to Moss, and that in turn triggered a stronger trust in my connection to the unseen.

MOSS

Moss shows the same early signs of psychic abilities that I did. He's currently 19-months old. It still amazes me daily that my husband and I created a body that harbors a soul. We gave a soul a home here on Earth. I think about this over and over but I still can't fully grasp the concept. It's beyond magical and I hope I never get over the extraordinary complexity of creating a tiny human through a process that occurred so naturally, with little involvement on my part. My body and his cells did all of the work. Procreation is proof of the intricate, intentional energetic magnitude of the universe.

I have tried to remain a neutral observer when it comes to the possibility of Moss having enhanced abilities. But the truth is, I hope that he does. I often wonder what would be different for me if I was raised in an environment where I was taught about the sacredness of connection to the unseen and given tools to integrate my experiences. Not that I fault my family in any way, but they didn't have the same understanding that I do having fully embraced my psychic self.

The first time Moss did something I questioned was psychic, I admittedly brushed it off as a wild coincidence.

My husband, Neil, my son, Moss, and I were all at the grocery store together. I was in the beverage aisle looking for my favorite drink that I like to buy as a little treat. I don't consume alcohol, so I sometimes like to have the equivalent of a "healthy" soda when my husband makes a cocktail. My favorite is a lemon-lime fizzy drink that can be hard to find as it's often sold out. I was searching up and down the aisle trying to scan every shelf for my soda. Moss and my husband were starting to struggle at the other end of the aisle and I felt myself rushing to find what I was looking for so we could move on. I gave up looking at the same time that my husband gave up the struggle with Moss.

"Mama," he called out as he walked towards me carrying a can.

I bent down to pick him up and it was my lemon-lime soda in his hands.

"Did you give him that?" I asked Neil, amused.

"No. He wouldn't put it down. I tried to make him put it back, but he was getting upset."

"Did you know this is what I was looking for?" I asked Neil.

"No. But I guess Moss did."

I recall thinking it was bizarre that he knew I wanted that. I could only remember having one or two of these sodas in his lifetime and didn't think he would have noticed or associated that drink with me. I even considered that I don't drink out of cans. I almost always pour my drinks into a glass. But he somehow knew. And he wasn't going to let it go until he delivered my soda.

Moss has also shown signs of telepathy. I'll be thinking of a person and something I need to text to them or do for them while my son is playing beside me. He'll look up from his game and say the person's name to me.

One day I was thinking of my husband and the tennis match he would be in that evening.

"Daddy," my son said to me.

"That's right baby," I confirmed to him. "Mommy is thinking about daddy."

My goal as a parent is to enhance his psychic self and teach him the beautiful things that can come from a pure, loving connection to spirit (if he is so inclined). I believe the world will become a better place if we ignite this truth in our younger generations and encourage them to both believe in it and trust in their senses. I will encourage Moss to enhance his imaginative abilities. And I will remain curious and engaged when he speaks of his "imaginary" experiences.

When Moss was a newborn, my father-in-law was perpetually concerned with how his hearing was developing. And for no apparent reason. Moss responded to sounds in a way I felt was normal and didn't show any signs of hearing difficulty. But my father-in-law constantly asked if he had his hearing checked yet. There was a small, worried part of me that was triggered by the thought of having his hearing documented and recorded in some kind of system. I don't openly discuss my experiences with testing in the schooling system. It's not exactly a coffee table chat kind of topic. Instead of sharing my fear and my hesitation, I decided to take Moss in for a hearing test.

I couldn't come up with any good excuses to appease my father-in-law without admitting my reluctance and the general uneasy feeling about organized, systemized testing of any sort. And besides, I can't really explain my childhood experience or any negative outcome from the testing. It just left me with a chronic, mild paranoia that psychic children are being tracked.

I made an appointment with the pediatrician when Moss was around 6-weeks old. When we got there, they laid him on a table and put a walkie talkie looking device near his head, pressed some buttons, and nonchalantly marked him down as "normal." I don't think I drew a single breath for the entire process. I was waiting, anxious and overly paranoid, for a head tilt from the tester, or some kind of odd reaction to his auditory response. I was worried that he would have the same heightened hearing abilities as me and that they would somehow be detected and recorded in a secret database somewhere to track him. But it was an uneventful experience. More than anything, it made me aware of the impact of my childhood testing experiences and my desire to protect my child from something I can't explain.

As he's aged, I've come to recognize that he does have the same keen sense of hearing as me. The first signs showed when he was around 6-months old. He would be scooting around on the floor, then lay his head to the side so that his ear was on the wooden surface. At first I brushed it off as him being tired. But after a few times watching him do it, I realized that he was listening to the vibrations from all around the house through the wood. We had a pier and beam foundation, where you could hear reverb from movements in other areas of the house if you got down there and listened. After I realized what he was doing, I would make little sounds for him by tapping my fingernails near his head or rolling a toy across the floor.

He was given a wooden train set with a small ramp for the train to travel up and over around the track. The first time I showed him how the train went fast on the way down the ramp, he squealed with excitement. Then he laid down beside the track, at the bottom of the ramp, and waited for me to do it again. His eyes were in line with the track and he placed his ear on the floor. He wanted to watch it and hear it.

He has a sharp awareness of aircraft and can detect from which direction planes and helicopters are approaching. This is harder than you may think. I try now, as an adult, to see if I can sense where the airplane is coming from based on the sound and it's difficult because we sometimes hear the echo of the sound and anticipate the plane from the opposite direction. I watch Moss when first hearing the aircraft and the majority of the time, he's waiting, eyes fixed on a particular spot in the sky, accurately spotting the plane overhead.

When he wakes in the night seeking comfort, he likes to lay across my chest with one ear in the cavity of my low sternum. I imagine what it would sound like for him. I'm fully aware that this is unlikely to be a unique experience for me as a mom and that instead, most mothers and babies experience bonds like this. What he's hearing is probably the same sounds that he experienced in the comfort of the womb. He falls deeply to sleep when I let him rest in this position.

The first time we moved Moss to his own room to sleep, I woke Neil about an hour later, in tears. I was exhausted and delirious from lack of sleep with a newborn. But even more troubling to me was the thought of Moss being alone if any visitors came. Neil left the room. I expected him to return with Moss within a few minutes but must have fallen asleep while waiting. I woke several hours later to find myself alone in our bedroom. I went searching. I entered the nursery, feeling a slight panic. Moss was sound asleep in his crib and my husband was asleep on the floor beside him. I woke Neil to ask what was going on. Neil told me that he wanted me to be able to rest, so he stayed with Moss so that I wouldn't worry about him being alone.

Time will tell what the future holds for all of us. The suspense is fascinating. I am anxious for him to speak someday soon and to share with us anything and everything he feels, senses, and remembers.

THE SESSION

That night from my childhood, when my sister and I experienced the bright lights and commotion—I decided to try a guided regression session to see if I could remember anything further about the experience.

I've worked with a regressionist several times throughout my journey to mediumship. Sometimes I am merely relaxed and recall every moment of the regression. Other times, I go into a complete blackout, only hearing myself afterwards through the recording the regressionist shares.

In the session I underwent to remember this evening, I was teetering the line of subtle awareness and a mental blackout. I waited several weeks post-session to review the recording. This is what I said while under hypnosis:

The lights and commotion were created to ensure everyone in the observable area was deeply asleep. My body was asleep, but I was wide awake. I could not move. Three beings entered my room. One tall, and faceless. The other two were shorter and wearing robes. I could not directly look at them, though I had complete control over my eyes. There was a black speaker-looking box placed in the corner of my room. The tall one picked up my limp body. I was three-years old. Then we simply vanished. We dematerialized.

I next see myself in a white, padded room. I am on a table and being inspected everywhere. I do not feel violated, but there are many different hands touching me. I get the sense that these hands are receptors, capable of transmitting data. There is a particular interest in my mouth and my teeth.

Then the memory flashes. I am looking face to face with a greenish-grey alien. I can see veins in its head. I sense that it is a male. It places one finger on my right collar bone and another on my left collar bone. Then there is the most loving connection I've ever experienced. I know this being.

The memory flashes. I see myself suspended in a circle of four other beings. I look down to my hands, they are foreign. A finger is missing and my thumb is the same length as the others. I scan my anatomy, then look at the four others, all standing in a circle. We are five. I am one of the five.

EPILOGUE

The (Never) End

Before ending the regression session, the hypnotist asked me if I'd like to see where I am from. I wanted to. I assumed it would be the land I remember as a gray being. But I traveled for millions, maybe even trillions of light years deeply into the vast void. There, I saw myself as a light. Both infinitesimally small and immeasurably massive. I was a brilliant shade of teal blue, and I had a recognizable love for adventure. It was as if I was made with the same vibratory frequency of adventure. This light was my starform, the essence that I believe I remain through each and every incarnation of life that I choose. And perhaps these incarnations are not occurring in sequential order, but instead, at once. That is the sense I had for each of us when I reconnected with my place of origin–my starform.

To every single reader who has made it through this entire journey with me, I thank you. I've felt a connection to you through my writing process. I've asked the loving guidance around me to help me produce the exact right words, to reach and affect the exact right people.

I feel you as I'm writing these final words. And when I close my eyes, I believe that I can see you. I see your beautiful, endless light.

ABOUT THE AUTHOR

Jackie Kenner

Jackie Kenner is an established Psychic Medium and Spiritual Business Consultant in Dallas, Texas. Before her current endeavors, Kenner pursued graduate studies at Macquarie University in Sydney, Australia. Her professional journey led her to New York City, where she spent over a decade serving in management consulting and operational capacities within the technology startup sphere.

With a wealth of experience, Kenner has guided numerous authors to successful publication, specializing in esoteric and spiritually-driven subjects. Her debut solo publication, Parked by the Exit, chronicles her transformative path to Psychic Mediumship. Kenner's literary contributions have been translated into multiple languages, including German, French, and Spanish.

Additionally, she is recognized as an Amazon Bestselling co-author of Project Starmaker, a compelling narrative exploring the realms between lives and the shadowy underpinnings of dark budget government programs.

For further insights into Jackie Kenner's work and to explore her other publications and services, visit her official website at www.jackiekenner.com.

Made in the USA
Coppell, TX
12 June 2024

33456476R00121